BAKING BY HAND

MAKE THE BEST ARTISANAL BREADS AND PASTRIES
BETTER WITHOUT A MIXER

ANDY &
JACKIE KING

FOUNDERS OF
A&J KING ARTISAN BAKERS

PAGE STREET
PUBLISHING CO.

PAGE STREET
PUBLISHING CO.

Copyright © 2013 Andy & Jackie King

First published in 2013 by
Page Street Publishing Co.
27 Congress Street, Suite 205-06
Salem, MA 01970
www.pagestreetpublishing.com

Distributed by Macmillan; sales in Canada by The Canadian Manda Group; distribution in Canada by The Jaguar Book Group.

16   15   14   13   1   2   3   4   5

ISBN-13: 978-1-62414-000-6
ISBN-10: 1-62414-000-9

Library of Congress Control Number: 2013936601

Cover and book design by Page Street Publishing Co.
Photography by Eric Laurits

Printed and bound in China

1%
FOR THE
PLANET
MEMBER

Page Street is proud to be a member of 1% for the planet. Members donate one percent of their sales to one or more of the over 1,500 environmental and sustainability charities across the globe who participate in this program. Since 2002 1% for the Planet has helped facilitate over $50 million in donations to these charities worldwide.

FOR MOON FACE AND PEA BRAIN,
AND FOR BANANA DOG—THE MOST PATIENT ONE OF ALL

CONTENTS

OUR BAKERY

It sounds like a silly coincidence or a fateful prognostication, but Jackie and I knew we were going to be bakers together from very early on. We had known each other for less than seven months, had recently starting dating, and Valentine's Day was coming up. Fantastic. I scrambled around to buy her a present, and settled on a great find from the local bookshop in Montpelier, Vermont, where we both were attending the New England Culinary Institute. We had connected over the simple things that let you know you're going to be with someone a while: food (obviously), a love of family, late nights watching the Game Show Channel, that immediate comfort that allows you to sit in silence and not feel weird about it. I knew I was going to marry her in about five minutes.

For Valentine's Day I bought Jackie a beautiful, large, coffee table book called *Artisan Baking* by Maggie Glezer. I met up with Jackie later in my little dorm-style bedroom to exchange presents. As I reached behind my back to present my gift, she did the same. We brought our gifts forth. And we both held the same present, with the exact same bookstore wrapping paper and ribbon.

It was clear that baking was in both of our bloods.

Fast forward four and a half years, and one of those books sat in our makeshift office, earmarked and dirty, along with some of the other invaluable reference books that helped us answer our own questions as we started a bakery. As much experience as you may think you have—and working for three and a half years at one of the best bakeries in the country, Portland, Maine's Standard Baking Co., gave us plenty of that—nothing prepares you for having to solve every problem yourself. These books kept our brains afloat. It was 2006, and we were up to our ears in dough, debt—and, thankfully, customers. Salem, Massachusetts, welcomed our little bakery with open arms, a steady stream of interested and open-minded locals allowing us to make it through that rough first year.

Jump forward another six and a half years, to the present. We've brought many of our books home from the bakery, as we've made so many mistakes and solved so many problems that we've discovered that now our experience is what's leading us. Our training, our research, just the day-to-day living with dough is what informs our decisions. We meet with our amazing bread and pastry bakers and talk about production and schedules and flavors, and we eat and argue and laugh, and then we get back to working and arguing and eating and laughing some more.

We love what we do: the passion, the people, the problem solving, the fun, the sweat, the end result. We just love to make and eat good food. When the act of dining starts to focus solely on the plate and less on the gathering of friends, that is bad. One of the reasons we love artisan bread is that, while it should be amazing on its own, it's also a perfect starting-off point for greater things. I'm not just talking about food—I'm talking about gathering those you care about near to you, facing one another and sharing a meal.

Once the loaf is made and sold, I want customers to come back and tell me what they did with it. I want to hear that it made an amazing bruschetta, or that it's the only sandwich bread little Delia will eat, or that you sawed some ciabatta in half and stuffed it with deli meats and sharp provolone to eat while watching football with the gang. I don't want to hear these things because I need to hear compliments about my product. I want to hear that it fulfilled its intended destiny as a canvas for your own food obsession.

WHAT GREAT BREAD IS, AND WHAT GREAT BREAD ISN'T

There is a vast canyon between a good loaf of bread and a bad one. They might all have the same ingredients, but you can spot a bad loaf just by looking at it. A pale, dull crust. Small, dense, a bit wonky on one side, no real definition to it. A quality loaf, however, is tall and proud, sporting a beautiful russet crust, a sharp burst or carefully slashed design. You can thump the bottom and hear that it has a nice, airy open crumb underneath a crackling crust with a matte sheen. It looks healthy and strong, and not least of all, delicious.

There's no magic to it, no secret ingredient to that second loaf, but the uninitiated are tempted to say that there is, and I don't blame them. There are few humbler food items than a loaf of bread, fewer still that are claimants of both the phrase *staff of life* and, in some circles, the title of *all that is unhealthy about your diet*. I find both positions a bit extreme and way too close to politicization. Making artisan bread isn't spell casting, it's not a statement, it's not part of a movement. It's a series of actions that create a final product that is greater than the sum of its parts, and therefore worth putting a bit of time into if one wants to understand the process.

And to those who claim that making a beautiful loaf of bread is an art: I humbly disagree. Our goal is to create a literal consumable; we want you to tear our product apart, not present it at a gallery. There are artistic elements to our baking, but most of those elements have functional purposes. The multicolored layering on a perfect croissant is a result of proper lamination (layering). The slashes on a loaf of North Shore Sourdough are there to carefully release expanding gasses from the loaf so as to achieve greater volume and uniform shape. The flour stencil of the turkey on the Thanksgiving Grand Levain is . . . well, okay, maybe that one is for fun. Take a photo of that bread and call *that* art. But if that loaf or that tart doesn't end up in someone's belly in short order, it hasn't fulfilled its purpose.

COMMITTING TO THE CRAFT:
BEING A BAKER, DESPITE THE HOURS

For whatever the reason, I've always been drawn to food traditions that have their roots deep in the culinary soil. Fermentation of all sorts (beer brewing, wine making and, of course, bread baking), working with active cultures, charcuterie and sausage making and cooking over open flame. Time-tested tradition and homage to the past have been hallmarks of almost everything I enjoy, from music to literature to cuisine. Jackie is the same way in her out-of-bakery endeavors (sled-dog running, vegetable gardening and raising farm animals, to name my favorites) and places great value and emphasis on family, hospitality and tradition. So it makes sense that we were both drawn to the warmth of the bake-shop early on in our culinary careers rather than to the tightly controlled chaos of your average kitchen line.

Baking is also a discipline that rewards not only careful attention to technique, but also supplemental research into the science of the craft. The baker relies on the healthy activity of the most basic forms of life to create the product and, therefore, a thorough understanding of how those organisms work (and under what conditions they thrive) can only benefit the artisan baker. There are scientific realities to why your bread is behaving the way it is, and most of them are easily understood and applied to your bakeshop, be it at home or at work. There are books and websites dedicated to food science—Harold McGee's *On Food and Cooking* is an essential read—and those who know the hows will most definitely know the whys. Baking can be as simple or as complicated as you want to make it, but the more you understand about the science of baking, the better a baker you'll be.

In baking, as in many other things, the simplest things are the proof of your talent. Judge an ice cream maker on the quality of his or her vanilla—there are no chunks of candy or fruit to cover up the ice cream base. If you want to understand the heart of a concert pianist, listen to how he or she treats the simplest sonata rather than a bombastic showpiece. Similarly, our bakers coax the most amazing baked goods out of most basic ingredients. Both the North Shore Sourdough and the ciabatta have almost the exact same contents, but their flavor profiles are miles apart. Why? Because when you apply science, knowledge, technique and tradition to simple ingredients, you can make them say a lot of different things.

SETTING UP SHOP

THE TOOLS TO TURN YOUR KITCHEN
INTO AN ARTISAN BAKESHOP

After years of working in professional kitchens, bakers begin to develop a particular sixth sense with regard to the atmosphere in which they'll be baking. Ours can see through that heat and seek out those areas in the kitchen that might be perfect for very particular tasks. They'll look for the corner near the window that might be 10 degrees cooler—a perfect place to store that bin of dough that came out a little warmer than expected. Through that swinging door is a spot in the hallway that's right under the AC vent, so we'll roll our rack of proofing Pain au Levain over there, or else it'll need to go in the oven just as the North Shore Sourdough is proofed and ready. That's one train wreck avoided.

The point is, great bakers know their kitchens. If they are baking in a foreign space, they'll take the time to evaluate the hot zones, the cool spots and those places that are just perfect for developing great bread.

Your kitchen is *your* bakery, and the first thing you need to do is to get to know it if you want to make great bread. You can cook a steak when the ambient temperature is 50°F/10°C or 100°F/40°C, and it won't make a difference in how long that steak needs to cook. If you were trying to make bread at 50°F/10°C and made no adjustments, you'd be waiting long into the night for that dough to ferment and proof. Make the same dough at 100°F/40°C, and you have yourself a fast-moving bread that may complete its life cycle in 6 hours. The atmosphere in your kitchen makes all the difference in the world, and it will be up to you to react accordingly. Great bakers are manipulators of variables first and foremost.

Being a great baker is about paying attention, and making adjustments based on your observations to produce dough that's at a good temperature for fermentation and proofing. It's a balancing act, and a little knowledge about the bread-making process will make a huge difference. Plus, we reveal plenty of the tricks up our sleeves that will give you a leg up on whatever your home bakery throws your way. But first, let us reintroduce you to your oven.

YOUR FRENCH-BUILT, STEAM-INJECTED, HEARTH STONE OVEN

If you've got one of these, feel free to skip ahead to the recipes. For the rest of us, it takes a little more rigging of our home ovens to produce the bread we like. At the moment, we own an inherited 15-year-old wall oven whose windows are susceptible to enthusiastically shattering when you look at them wrong. The good news is that every one of these recipes was developed using that exact piece-of-junk oven, so rest assured that they will work in whatever you've got. Great technique and good decisions can trump any "unique" piece of equipment you own.

Even so, everyone's oven needs a little help to turn it into an artisan bread-baking powerhouse. You need just three items:

BAKING STONE

The bigger and thicker, the better. A round pizza stone works fine for one loaf at a time, but we prefer one of the square ones that takes up an entire rack. We can fit two or three loaves on it at once, and it most closely resembles the baking surface we have at the bakery. If you're getting one for the first time and you want to make sure it'll last forever, we suggest the FibraMent baking stones, by AWMCO—they have sizes for all ovens and are ¾-inch/2-cm thick. That's about as heavy as you can get them. Arrange your baking racks so that you have one as close to the bottom element as possible. If your oven doesn't have a bottom element, drop the stone right on the floor. That's where your baking stone is going to live. We keep ours in the oven at all times, as it moonlights as a roasted potato crisper, a piecrust setter, a thin-crust pizza stone and generally creates much more even heat throughout the oven at all times, provided you preheat your oven for the appropriate temperature at least an hour before baking. Those stones take a while to heat up, but they retain that heat longer. That's the key.

CAST-IRON PAN

You can find one of these heavy, thick frying pans for almost nothing at barn sales or in the back room of any antique store. Barring that, any good hardware store will carry a selection in its kitchenware section. You'll want to dedicate this pan for steam generation, because it will tend to get rusty as time goes on; that's why it's nice to get an old, used one and brush it off a bit. Your steam generator (See? It's not even a pan anymore!) will live on the top rack of your oven, far enough away from the baking stone that the dough has enough headspace to rise and color, but not so jammed up there that you can't slide it in and out easily. Your oven's default rack positions will dictate exactly where everything goes, but just as long as you can fit both your stone and your steam generator in, you're good to go.

WATER MISTER

Used in conjunction with the cast-iron pan, a water mister is great for spritzing your oven just as you load in all of the bread, and then again a few minutes later. Again, this ensures that your bread is rising in a humid environment and that you're getting the most out of your oven spring.

OTHER ITEMS TO HELP YOU BAKE GREAT BREAD

I used to be a terrible handyman. Pretty much everything I tried to cut, plumb, unscrew, build or assemble turned out to be an abject disaster. Basically, what I learned from many, many similar experiences (and, thankfully, no lost digits) is that it's really important to have the correct tools for the job you're trying to accomplish.

The same is true with baking equipment. There are certain items that will make your life a heck of a lot easier if you equip yourself with them. **We've tried to arrange these in order of importance, so you can have a priority list to work from.** They're not too expensive individually, but buying them all at once might be a bit daunting. At home we keep everything in a big plastic tub with a cover in the basement, and then haul it all up on baking days.

DIGITAL SCALE

A must-have. Get one that measures in grams as well as pounds and ounces and that has a tare function (which allows you to subtract the weight of the container); there are many reasonably priced, good-quality scales on the market. To make great bread, you must weigh ingredients because it's far more precise. A cup of tightly packed flour weighs a lot more than a cup of fluffed-up flour, and those ounces could make all the difference between a nice, open crumb and a tight, cottony one. Never trust a bread recipe that gives measures in volume. Ever.

Digital Scale

DIGITAL THERMOMETER

Don't trust your Spidey-sense. Correct temperatures are very, very important.

HEAT LAMP

As we've mentioned before, one of the biggest hurdles to great home baking is that rarely do home kitchens mimic the hot and humid, yeast-friendly environment of the bakeshop. One spring we were setting up a new home for some baby chicks that would be arriving the next day. To keep them warm we set up a long-corded heat lamp that can be adjusted up or down to create the optimal temperature. The connection was pretty obvious. One extra heat lamp later, and we could raise active dough (and more chickens!) in the dead of winter. It's a pretty simple setup. See ours below.

FISH TUBS

We know it sounds strange. At the bakery, we use commercial bus tubs to hold our dough, because they keep the dough in a nice, rectangular shape that's easy to divide. Fish tubs are just smaller versions, perfect for the home baker, and you can flip them over and use them as makeshift proofing boxes. They're especially useful in croissant production, where you need a nice, rectangular

Digital Thermometer

Heat Lamp

dough into which to roll your butter. These things are available most easily, not coincidentally, at your local fish store. Just ask the fellow in charge if they have a few deep ones (the shallow tubs won't work) that you can buy, and after a thorough cleaning, you'll have yourself a stack of perfect dough bins.

BOWL SCRAPERS

Know what's not useful for scraping bowls? Your fingertips. So, while flexible plastic bowl scrapers are not essential, they are really useful. They curve right around the inside of your bowl so you can make sure you're combining all of those dry ingredients with the wet. They're also very useful for cleaning your bowls out, because a starter stuck to the sides of a bowl is like glue when it dries.

BENCH BRUSH

For brushing flour off your work space bench and dough. Get the softest bristles you can. A clean bench is an organized bench!

PROOFING BOARD AND COUCHE

We proof on 18-inch × 26-inch/45 cm × 66-cm wooden boards (sometimes called "bagel boards"). You can make a proofing board out of anything you want: the back of a sheet pan, a piece of plywood or plastic and so on. You'll also want a piece of canvas called a *couche* (that's French for "diaper") if you're planning on making baguettes or batards. They're available at specialty baking websites (see Sources, page 236). You might even be able to find a suitable replacement at a fabric store. They should be the same width as, and about twice the length of, your proofing board.

Proofing Board and Couche

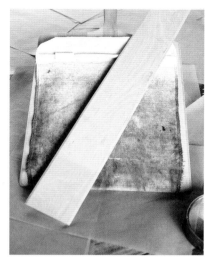

Bannetons/Proofing Baskets   *Lame and Razors*   *Peel*

BANNETONS/PROOFING BASKETS

Many of the shapes in the book are made using proofing baskets. We order ours in bulk from Germany, but they're available from specialty bread websites. When in a pinch, a smooth, floured towel lining a bowl will work.

LAME AND RAZORS

A lame (pronounced "lahm") is a long piece of metal onto which a razor blade is attached, and that entire unit is used to slash your bread. You can purchase the lame frame and the blades separately (allowing for easy razor switch-out when the blade gets dull), or you can order special preassembled lames. Either works just fine.

PEEL

A wooden board for sliding your bread into and out of the oven. It's definitely the most recognizable baker thing you'll have in your kitchen (especially if you hang it from the wall), so if you want a nice wooden one, go nuts. You can also place your bread on the back of a floured sheet pan and slide it into the oven that way, but really, the peel is pretty badass. Seriously, get the peel.

TOOLS FOR SUPERIOR PASTRY MAKING

ROLLING PIN

You probably have one of these, but make sure you have a heavy one; otherwise, put it on your Father's or Mother's Day gift list. You'll need the weight to stretch out your laminated doughs as the folds make them tighter and tighter.

PIZZA WHEEL

For quick cutting of croissants and pastry dough. I got yelled at in culinary school for calling these things "pizza wheels" instead of "pastry wheels," so now that we're writing a book on pastry and bread, we're calling them "pizza wheels." Take *that,* Chef!

CROISSANT WHEEL

If you find yourself making lots and lots of plain croissants, you might want to invest in one of these. It's like a rolling pin, but rather than a wood roller, there are sharp metal cutters in the shape of croissants. Just roll along your strip of dough and voilà—instant triangles, ready to be shaped. They run a little pricey and come in various sizes, so make sure you're committed before you invest in one.

CAKE RINGS/CIRCLE CUTTERS

These are useful for all sorts of pastry tasks—cakes (duh), quiche, mousse and so forth. They're sturdy and stainless steel, so they'll last forever. We use

Pizza Wheel

Croissant Wheel

Cake Rings/Circle Cutters/Flan Rings

them to quickly cut out circles of dough, especially handy in high-volume situations. But even at home, if you're tired of using pan lids and dinner plates (which we've done many, many times), these will make your pastry life much easier. Get rings in sizes of 12, 10, 7, 6 and 5 inches/30, 25, 18, 15 and 12 cm, and you'll have a nice set.

BAKING MOLDS, FLAN RINGS, PIE PANS, STICKY BUN TINS AND SO ON

Although there are some pastry products we make that, like bread, go right on the baking stone, generally speaking you'll need something in which to hold your pastry creation. Some things you can get at the grocery store—we got our sticky bun tins at Dawson's Hardware, down the street. For others, you might have to hit up a larger big-box store, and for things like flan rings, you'll likely have to visit a pastry supply website (see Sources, page 236).

The flan rings are especially important for many of our sweet and savory tarts, so if those recipes are in your sights, purchase six 5-inch/12-cm rings and one 8-inch/20-cm ring right off the bat.

Deep mini pie tins (5-inches/12-cm diameter by 1-inch/2.5-cm deep) can be purchased online or (again) in box homeware stores or at well-stocked hardware stores. We like our ceramic pie plates to be as deep as you can get them—thin pies have no place in our home.

Fluted pastry molds (4 inches/10 cm) can generally be purchased at the large box homeware stores or online from specialty retailers.

SHEET PANS

The best sheet pans to use are the largest, heaviest-duty ones you can find, preferably ones that are 13 inches × 18 inches/33 cm × 45 cm. All sheet pans are not created equal—the thinnest ones bend and warp at higher temperatures, creating rivers of fruit juice or other liquids that puddle in the corners of the pan. It's worth the extra few bucks to get the thick ones.

COOLING RACKS

Both pastry and bread like to cool suspended off the counter to maximize air flow. Things tend to steam and soften when sitting on solid surfaces.

PARCHMENT PAPER

Baking on nonstick parchment makes cleanup a snap. You can purchase precut half-sheet-pan-size packs online. (We won't go into get into how angry we get trying to rip a perfect size off of one of those stupid rolls.)

ESSENTIAL INGREDIENTS FOR GREAT ARTISAN BREAD AT HOME

Knowledge is king in the bakeshop, and we're constantly talking about why products come out good (or bad). We can't stress enough the importance of knowing how your ingredients interact with one another and what you can do to increase the instances of positive interaction.

We're not asking you to get a master's degree in bread science, but the following info will help you understand those whys a little better, will make you a more capable baker and will result in a great loaf of bread. And that's the goal, isn't it? Increase your knowledge, increase your reward.

Please keep in mind that when we refer to "ingredient percentages" here, we do the funny baker thing of expressing percentages in relation to the flour. So, if we're talking about 60 percent water in a dough, that means 100 pounds/45 kg of dough gets 60 percent water. That's just how we roll.

THE BONES OF WONDERFUL BREAD

Wheat flour is the most important part of your bread; flour is also the most complicated part of your bread. We're going to keep it simple, as there are other books that go into the wonderful world of protein analysis, flour content analysis and flour quality analysis. And, the odds are, you're not going to have that much of a choice when picking flour up at your local grocery store. If you're interested, (see Sources page 236) for books that will steer you down that interesting but complex path.

Standard wheat flour is graded by its protein content: The higher the protein percentage, and thus the percentage of gluten in the flour, the stronger the dough will be. The stronger the dough is, the more likely it is to trap gas and have a nice rise.

So, here's how it works at the supermarket: *cake flour* or *pastry flour* is low protein/low strength to help increase the tenderness of pastry products. *Bread flour* is high protein/high strength to allow for a chewy crumb, strong crust and maximum rise. *All-purpose flour* splits the difference, which is fine for most pastry products but not optimal for artisan bread production. **We use bread flour for all of our breads in this book, and all-purpose flour for all of the pastry.**

One final note: Be sure to buy unbleached, unbromated flour. In a nutshell, it's less tampered with by the manufacturer, less altered with chemicals and generally less scary.

OTHER FLOURS

There are myriad flours you can use to augment your baking, some of which are wheat derivatives, like semolina and kamut, and some of which are other cereal grains, like corn and rye. Each has individual effects on the quality of the dough into which you mix it. Rye, for example, tends to absorb a ton of water and makes a dough notice-ably stickier. Corn just absorbs water, adding nothing in terms of strength. One particular item of note: Any time you're adding an additional grain to your mix, it will most likely work to break down the gluten structure of your dough and make it less strong. This is due to the little bits of corn, rye husk or semolina acting like little knives that cut the dough open as it rises, so take care when shaping and rising these types of doughs.

If you're using extra grains in creating your own recipe, they shouldn't make up much more than 20 percent of your total flour weight. Larger amounts will significantly affect your dough development, which is fine, but it might take more experimentation to create a great loaf.

CONTROLLING THE FEEL OF YOUR DOUGH WITH WATER

Water temperature is the primary way we control initial dough temperature and, obviously, how we hydrate the flour. As a reference, 60 percent hydrated dough is very dry and tight, while an 85 percent hydrated dough is very loose.

FROM SEA TO TABLE: SALT BRINGS IT ALL TOGETHER

In addition to adding flavor, salt serves to tighten the gluten structure of your developing dough. You'll notice that as soon as you add your salt to your mix and work it in, the dough will start pulling away from the bowl. That's why we add it after the initial resting period (the autolyse). Otherwise, it would tighten up the dough and make it harder for the protein to absorb water. Unless other salty ingredients are included in your recipe, your salt percentage should be a solid 2 percent of dough weight. We prefer to use fine sea salt in all of our breads at home for two reasons: It dissolves into the dough much more easily than does kosher or other coarser salt, and we just like the fact that it comes from the ocean. Scientifically speaking, though, sea salt and mined table salt are both pretty much sodium chloride. When we want larger crystals of salt on a focaccia or a savory tart, however, we go with your traditional kosher salt. If you're not picky, use what you have on hand.

Here's a basic rule for converting fine sea salt from measuring spoon units to grams, and vice versa:

1 teaspoon fine sea salt = 7 g
1 tablespoon fine sea salt = 21 g

COMMERCIAL YEAST: EASIEST WITH INSTANT

There are three types you can buy: *fresh yeast*, which comes in "cakes;" *active dry yeast*, which needs to be activated with warm water to work; and *instant yeast* (also called "Rapid Rise™"), which can just be added to the mix. There is no discernible difference in the final product, whichever you use. We use instant yeast here at the bakery because of its stability and ease of use, and **all of the recipes in this book use instant** as well. But, if you want to use another kind, or it's all you have on the shelf, here are the conversion factors:

Instant yeast to fresh yeast: multiply by 1.34

Instant yeast to active dry yeast: multiply by 3.19 (Just remember: Active dry yeast needs to be activated in warm water before incorporating. The package should have instructions.)

Here's a basic rule for converting instant yeast from measuring spoon units to grams, and vice versa:

1 teaspoon instant yeast = 4 g
1 tablespoon instant yeast = 12 g

COMMERCIAL STARTERS: GETTING A JUMP ON GREAT FLAVOR

Because the essence of artisan baking is slow and low, it makes sense that it would be a boon to the dough to start it well ahead of the final mix. We have two primary starters that we use in our mixes, and they're differentiated solely by their hydration levels. Take a portion of total water in the mix and a portion of your total flour, spike it with yeast and get that baby bubbling away 12 hours ahead of time. When the time comes to mix the dough, you'll have developed a ton of organic acids that will heighten the depth of flavor, increase the dough strength and lengthen the dough's shelf life (much like sourdough does). These acids are at the heart of artisan baking, and their development is primarily why it takes so long to make our products.

We primarily use two different types of commercial starters at the bakeshop and at home, and both are defined by how much they are hydrated. A *poolish* is a traditional French starter that is 100 percent water, and is named after the Polish, though no one can really explain why. Remember those strange bakers' percentages and how they're based on the percentage of flour? That 100 percent means that it has exactly the same amount of water as flour. This adds strength and flavor to the dough. We generally use a poolish in doughs that have a lower percentage of water in the final recipe, to encourage a large, open crumb.

A *biga* has Italian origins, so we use it in our ciabatta and other wetter doughs to add a bit more structure throughout the process. It typically is 60 percent water, making it a much stiffer starter than the sloppier poolish.

And, although we don't use any in this book, a simple way of adding flavor to a dough is to use what we call *pate fermente*—literally, "fermented dough." Just save a chunk of French or ciabatta dough from a mix in a bag in your fridge, and work it into any new dough you're making within a week or so. Voilà, instant starter.

SOURDOUGH STARTERS

We've written a whole chapter on sourdough and how you can make a starter yourself, but the basic deal is that it's a symbiotic mixture of wild yeast and bacteria, suspended in water and fed the starches in flour. See Chapter 4 for all the details.

YOUR HANDS

THE MOST IMPORTANT TOOL IN YOUR KITCHEN

Cooks have their knives, bakers have their hands. For the baker, there is no length of wood and steel between the product and the person during production. The list of things bakers do with their fingers is unending: They detect strengths and weaknesses, tiny defects in the dough and temperature; they tap the bottom of a loaf to determine doneness, catch things falling off the peel and on and on and on.

On my second or third shift at my first baking job, a seasoned baker asked, "How does the dough feel today?" I answered, "It feels a lot like dough to me." I had no frame of reference for what was good or bad, tight or loose, warm or cold. That comes only with experience. Because the more you bake, the more you feel the dough with your hands and see the results that arise from any particular batch of dough, the more you will be able to recognize what proper mixes feel like. Even today, as we walk around the bakery we reach into bins to poke the contents, run our hands over proofing loaves and grab handfuls of not-yet-finished dough still in the big mixer. It informs us and reconnects us with the day's work, and lets us keep tabs on the progress of the bread cycle.

Bake enough, and your dough will tell you exactly how it's doing right when you lay your hands on it.

Here are the keys to the baking process that will result in great bread on a more consistent basis. At the bakery we call this the Cycle, and as an experienced baker, you will begin to see every dough in terms of where it is in its own Cycle. Knowing the life cycle of your bread will allow you to understand why it acts the way it does.

SCALING IN WEIGHT, NOT VOLUME

This is bakeshop-speak for weighing your ingredients. We rarely use volume measurements, because a dry ingredient's weight will vary depending on how it's packed into the cup. If you dig into a fresh bag of flour that's been on the shelf for a while, it will have settled into a compact mass. It's much more accurate to weigh everything in pounds and ounces (kilograms and grams), dry and wet alike; even liquids have varying densities that may affect how your dough behaves.

If you want to get your great bread off on the right foot, scale carefully, and without distraction! We put our mixing room in a little private corner of the bakery so our folks won't get distracted, and our cooking school had an enforced rule: *Don't talk to the mixer when he or she is scaling.*

MIXING BY HAND MAKES YOU A BETTER BAKER

We have nothing against electric mixers. We use them all the time at the bakery. They're big, heavy, cast-iron models that can mix a couple hundred pounds of dough at a time (and those are the small commercial bread mixers!) and, most important, are designed for the express purpose of mixing dough in bakeries like ours—establishments that push out way more dough than you ever will in your home kitchen.

But when we're talking about making dough in 4-pound or 5-pound/1.5 or 2-kg batches, we use it as an opportunity to create bread using the most traditional method possible. There is no replacing the experience of starting your dough, the one that you will walk through its entire life cycle, with your own two hands. Feel the gluten develop between your fingers, push and knead until the liquid is absorbed, incorporate the yeast and salt with your fingers. It's the joy of being a bread baker.

So that mixer you have on your counter should really be pushed aside when you're thinking of making bread at home. You'll need the counter space for folding, dividing and shaping your loaves.

HAND-MIXING TECHNIQUE

1. Combine all your flours in a bowl (but no salt or instant yeast).

2. Put your water and starter (sourdough or otherwise) in a bowl large enough to mix your dough without it spilling over the side.

3. Add your flours to the water/starter mixture. Holding the side of the bowl in your nondominant hand, press your dominant hand into the middle of the mixture with an open palm. Squeeze your fist and turn your hand over. Repeat this action all along the edges of the bowl, turning the bowl in between each squeeze—the goal is not only to hydrate the dough completely, but also to incorporate the entire starter into the dough evenly.

4. When the dough starts to come together and build strength, start scooping the dough from the sides and into the middle of the dough and pushing down, turning the bowl the entire time. You want to bring the dough to a shaggy mass stage, where all the liquid is incorporated, but very little gluten has developed.

5. Let the shaggy mass rest for 30 minutes. This is what bakers call the autolyse—a period of resting when the barely developed gluten strands absorb the liquid in the mix, reducing the necessary amount of final mixing.

6. Sprinkle salt and dry yeast (if necessary) into the surface of the dough. Again gripping the bowl with your nondominant hand and continuously turning, grab the dough from the sides of the bowl and push toward the middle for about a minute, or until the yeast and salt are completely incorporated and the dough is a cohesive mass that you can pick up in one go, if you wanted to. At this point, if you have additions like nuts or fruit, add them and continue mixing to incorporate.

Cover the dough, and place it in the warmest spot in your kitchen.

THE FERMENTATION PROCESS

When the dough is sitting in its bowl in that time between the mixing and the divide, we call that the bulk fermentation. That's what's going on: The yeast is eating the starches and sugars in the flour, producing carbon dioxide and inflating pockets in the gluten structure like a million tiny balloons inflating at once. If we're using commercial yeast, we'll generally go with a 2-hour fermentation period, due to the more predictable nature of the leavener. We'll give almost every pure sourdough an extra hour of fermentation to give the homegrown microorganisms a bit longer to get a head of steam up. And while those yeasts chomp away at the starch and break down that gluten structure you're starting to form, it's important that you continue to build more dough strength. The best way to do that is using our 30-minute four-fold technique, which we use throughout this book.

THE FOUR-FOLD TECHNIQUE: THE KEY TO GREAT DOUGH MADE AT HOME

This is really the crux of building good dough strength at home. Rather than kneading and kneading and kneading the dough at the mixing stage, it is more beneficial to most dough (and to most home bakers) to develop its strength over the course of the entire fermentation period. By giving the dough a series of timed folds interspersed by periods of rest, we can build a beautifully developed dough while monitoring its progress throughout the fermentation period. And it's incredibly easy, it keeps you in touch with your dough as it moves along so that you can learn from it and it makes great bread. Here's how it works:

1. Using your fingers or a bowl scraper, gently turn the dough out onto a floured counter.

2. Using the pads of your fingers (not the sharper tips), grasp the left side of the dough and bring it about two-thirds of the way across the rest of the dough. Brush away any excess flour that may have come from the table. Do the same for the right side.

3. Bring the bottom section up toward the middle and, finally, bring the top down. Roll the dough over so the seam is on the bottom, and place it back into the bowl. Return it to its warm spot.

4. Repeat this procedure every 30 minutes until the bulk fermentation is complete, according to your recipe.

That's pretty much it. Can't you just feel that gluten developing and fermentation chugging away right under your fingertips? That's the stuff of life right there.

The rest of the dough's life before shaping is fairly self-explanatory. Dividing your dough into the desired weights is your first interaction with your fully fermented dough. At this point it will be soft, warm and strong, starting its transformation into a loaf of bread. Most recipes call for a "bench rest," which is transitional shape from sloppy cut piece to final shape. That shouldn't take more than 20 or 30 minutes, and in some cases, like the Ciabatta, there is no bench rest at all. Each recipe's instructions will tell you whether it's necessary or not.

Finally, you're on to shaping.

SHAPE UP: SIMPLE TECHNIQUES TO ACHIEVE BEAUTIFULLY SHAPED LOAVES

After the mix and the folds, the shape is the most important technique the home baker can learn to achieve bakery-style bread at home. There are myriad shapes to choose from, and bakers all over the world pride themselves in expertly crafting loaves that burst beautifully in the oven. We're going to focus on four basic shapes, all of which can be applied to almost any recipe in the book. We give our suggestions for each loaf, but feel free to experiment.

THE ROUND

Starting with one side of the divided piece, gently but firmly fold and roll the dough up while turning it to create a roundish shape. It's more like you're using your two hands to gather a seam together at the bottom. Using the table for grip, pull the dough back toward you, stretching the surface tight.

THE BATARD

Fold the left and right bottom "corners" of the round on top of each other, creating a bell shape. From the bottom, roll up the dough, pulling back and stretching the surface as you go. When you get to the end, use your fingers to pinch the seam along the table you now have a cylinder shape. For a "stubbier" version, gather the sides in more as you shape. For a longer batard, roll the sides with your hands to taper the ends.

THE FENDU

Dust your work surface with a good amount of flour, and gently scoop your rounded loaves up with your bench knife and place seam side down on the flour. Sprinkle some flour on the top of the loaf as well. Grab the thinnest rolling pin you have, such as a French one or a 1-inch/2.5-cm diameter dowel, and press down in the middle of the loaf. Remove the pin to reveal a bisected loaf. Roll the two sides together, gently flip the loaf over and place cut side down in the banneton.

THE BAGUETTE

Pre-shape your dough into loose cylinders. Covering and cooling the dough at this point helps with shaping, as it reduces activity and allows you to more easily stretch the dough. Then 30 to 60 minutes in the refrigerator or out on a cold porch should do the trick.

Flip your pre-shape onto your work surface—use very little flour. Fold the bottom third of your loaf into the middle, and pat down. Fold the top third of the loaf into the middle as well, and pat down again. Leading with your nondominant hand and going from the bottom up, roll the dough three-quarters of the way onto itself and seal it with the heel of your dominant hand—that's right to left if you're right-handed. Repeat this motion again, this time sealing the seam against the table with the heel of your hand. Then, using firm but even pressure with both hands, simultaneously stretch and roll the baguette out to the sides, stopping when it reaches 12 inches to 15 inches/ 30 to 40 cm. Lay the baguette onto your couche seam side up, and pleat it; that is, grab opposite sides of the couche with your fingers and "pinch up" a little cloth wall between the loaves.

  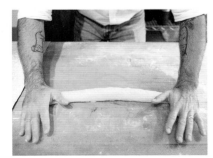

KNOW THE SCORE: SLASHING FOR THE PERFECT BURST

Slashing achieves two purposes: it releases pressure as the dough is peeled into the oven, creating a loaf of maximum volume as the "oven spring" occurs, and it makes beautifully decorative ears and patterns on the loaf's surface. Some patterns are dictated by tradition, like the distinctive baguette, and others will be up to your own creativity.

The angle of the blade will determine whether the slash just falls open or results in a distinctive "ear."

90°: Will open loaf up with no burst

45°: Will achieve a nice burst on a larger loaf, like a sourdough boule or batard

30°: Will achieve a burst on a smaller, thinner loaf, like a baguette

90°

45°

30°

THE PM BREAD BAKER

SOURDOUGH, GRAINS AND HYBRIDS

I got into baking and got out of restaurant cooking early. There was just something about working with dough that grabbed hold of my brain and wouldn't let go. But, if there's a shift at the bakery that most resembles working on the line at a fancy bistro, it's the PM bake. Apart from the hours being similar (2 or 3 p.m. until whenever you're done cleaning), the rhythm of the days, the peak of hustle and the running-on-fumes denouement of switching off the lights mirror each other nicely. The baker arrives, checks the night's numbers and prep list, determines the correct order of operations, sets up racks and bannetons—the baker's mise en place—roasts garlic, dices apricots and grabs a coffee as the mix begins.

About 2 hours in, things start to heat up. Doughs are up, dividing begins and it's all kinetic energy from there on out. Friday night service? It's nonstop, hot in front of the oven, keep hydrating, where's my lame, empty the trash, rotate the dough, that damn levain better be out of the oven in 40 minutes or I'm dead, sneak into the walk-in to cool off. Then comes the cleaning, then cleaning some more, then it's over. Then comes the beer, and Lord, I need a shower.

> " The thing I love about my shifts is that I can see a project from start to finish every day. In each shift I've got a new set of problems to solve, but when it comes down to it, the process is the same. As night bakers, we've got about 5 hours to invest in the sourdoughs before proofing. Sure, we use this time to mix, fold, cut and shape, but also to dance with it (sometimes literally). If we pay close enough attention, we can feel what the dough needs and work with it. Whether that means moving it between rooms for temperature control, adding more flour or listening to more Queen. My best day is when I'm working a big farmers' market bake in the middle of summer, thermostat reads 90 degrees, my dough feels overhydrated, I'm sweating my ass off and I pull my bread out of the oven and it's picture perfect. The bursts, the color, the shape. It means I did the dance correctly. "

JESS LEMIRE
PM Baker

SOURDOUGH

On my first day of training at the Standard Baking Co., I grabbed a freshly baked sourdough boule on my way out the door. It was on this long walk home through the summer crowds of Portland, Maine, that I fully realized the power of a loaf of freshly baked bread; short of walking our Labrador puppy through a preschool, I'm not sure what I could have done to receive more attention than I did that night. Folks just love a nice loaf of sourdough. Despite the occasional "I don't like sourdough!" comments we get at the bakery—to which my response usually is "No, you don't like *bad* sourdough. "—they are the loaves that the real bread lovers gravitate toward. Nothing makes me happier than someone coming in first thing in the morning and ordering a cup of coffee and a beautifully burst, deeply caramelized boule. *That's* a bread lover.

It's probably this deep love for the complex tang of sourdough that has led to the somewhat ridiculous mythos surrounding it. Bakers likely feed them twice a day, keep them warm and safe, name them silly names . . . To be honest, they're very much like pets. Heck, if you can call sea monkeys pets, I think *saccharomyces cerevisiae* and *lactobacilli* can also be honored with that title. The difference is, the sea monkeys sit on your shelf and eventually are spilled by your little brother. The yeast culture can produce bread to which your friends and customers will become addicted. Hence, the reverence.

But, on the other side of the coin sit all of those other crackpot theories on sourdough starter. I've heard everything from "You can't ever wash the bucket it lives in or the whole thing will die" to "I can get you real San Francisco sourdough starter here on the East Coast." None of that is true. Washing the bucket won't do it much harm. I've restarted my starter from a small trace of it in our rinse sink when I realized I had dumped it down the drain before making a backup. I've kept it frozen for years, only to thaw it out and have it start foaming away in my sink. I've forgotten to feed it for days on end, and watched it bounce back with just a couple of refresher meals. It's pretty resilient stuff! It will survive in your kitchen just fine.

It's also incredibly local. Any sourdough starter grown and maintained in your house will have a distinct flavor profile, as the local bacteria to your region will be the organisms that produce the sour flavor in your dough. San Francisco contains some local flora that produced a tang so unique it was named *lactobacillus sanfranciscensis*. Despite its fame, however, that poor, homesick bacteria will be overtaken by the local cultures when it is brought eastward and fed and maintained. Thus, it's impossible to have a true San Francisco sourdough here on the East Coast.

Last, sourdough starter is incredibly easy to make. It's got two basic ingredients: flour and water. It takes a bit of time and monitoring, but if you plan it out a couple of weeks in advance, you'll have a starter that you can pass on to your kids.

All sourdough starters are really the same thing: a balanced symbiosis of wild yeast and bacteria suspended in a mixture of flour and water. The yeasts are harvested from healthy flour when the culture is first developed; the bacteria is floating all around us as we speak and is attracted to the culture as it develops; the flour serves as food, and the water is the medium through which the yeast move to snack on the starches in the flour. If you remember 10th grade bio lab, you'll recall that starches are basically carbohydrates, which are strings of glucose molecules.

See where we're going? Feed sugar to yeast and you have one of the most basic biological processes—fermentation. It's what drives everything we as bakers do, and that's why we're touching on it here. How does it apply to home baking? If your kitchen is too cold, your yeast is sluggish and not eating your flour fast enough. Slow fermentation! If you throw your loaf in the oven and it collapses into a deflated heap, you let the yeast eat through too much of the gluten structure—the flour. Too much fermentation! If your loaf comes out perfectly proofed, you've let the yeast break down your dough just enough to open up that crumb but keep its shape. Nice fermentation, buddy!

So remember this: If you don't know how to properly ferment, you don't know how to bake bread. Controlling your atmosphere, adjusting your temps, mixing by hand and folding your dough are all ways of managing the snacking of your single-celled organism collection.

> " The first day I worked at the bakery, Andy pulled a large bucket down from a shelf and made me take a sniff out of it. The smell was vinegary and yeasty and sour. The surface was wobbly and studded with bubbles like a tiny albino swamp.
>
> When he had finished explaining the starter's feeding schedule, I recalled something I'd read about a beehive. At any given moment, there are one or two baby bees being fed exclusively on this cream-of-the-crop pollen called royal jelly, so when the queen keels over, after giving birth to her billionth baby, they have the fattest, most awesome baby bee ready to take her place.
>
> The bubbles alone looked enough like honeycomb for the similarity to get lodged in my head, and I remember Andy's face when I said, "Oh! Like a baby bee!" He smiled and nodded.
>
> As I mixed the the starter the next day, all I could think about were fat little baby bees. So it stuck. Baby Bee. "

JESSICA MANN
PM Baker

By the way, the same is true for doughs made with commercial yeast. You're just using harvested yeast specially developed for baking rather than wild yeast. So keep that in mind when making the baguettes, ciabatta and all those nonsourdough breads in this book, okay?

Also, the fun stuff: You can name your sourdough starter whatever you want. When visiting chefs, bakers and home enthusiasts stop into the bakery, they'll usually ask where the "mother" is, or the "chef," the "levain," or whatever it is they call their culture where they bake. People often ask where ours came from, as if I'm going to reveal that I pulled it from a flaming crevasse on the side of Mt. Poilane. Fact is, I developed our sourdough culture on the counter of a very normal family kitchen, in very normal bowls and with very regular feedings. And I didn't name it. I wanted my future bakers, the ones who would be responsible for the day-to-day production in the bakery, to have that honor as they developed the special bond that all bakers have with those little creatures that raise their dough to such heights. So our sourdough starter is called the Baby Bee. Why? See above.

STARTING AT THE SOURDOUGH

The equipment, ingredients and time involved in starting your own sourdough culture are minimal. You'll need:

Two containers. Make them big enough to hold the starter, taking into account that it will, at some point, be expanding as it ferments. You also don't want them to be too large, or the starter will just be a thin layer on the bottom. Plastic quart=liter-size containers worked great for me.

A spoon. Or something to stir with. Or your hands.

A scale. Weigh all ingredients. Weigh all ingredients. *Weigh all ingredients.*

Unbleached, unbromated white flour. This is the food for your growing culture, so you want it to be as untreated as possible. Remember, bleaching is just a way to make flour look whiter by using lovely chemicals Don't feed it to your yeast, or for that matter, your family, okay?

Whole rye flour, preferably organic. Whole rye has a higher nutritional content than white flour and will make for a more appealing environment in which wild yeasts and bacteria will thrive. Getting the organic stuff will ensure that it has not been chemically altered or enhanced in any way. It's not completely necessary, but it may speed the process along.

Dechlorinated water. When you're just getting started, it's best to give the yeast every possible advantage. If your tap water smells like the YMCA pool like ours does, it's a good idea to let it sit in an open container overnight to disperse some of that chlorine. If you forgot to do that and you're raring to make starter, a gallon of bottled water from the store will get you a week or so into making your culture. At that point, the culture should be booming and won't be harmed by what comes out of any home's tap.

DAY 1:

6 oz/170 g white bread flour

6 oz/170 g whole rye flour (organic preferred)

12 oz/340 ml distilled or dechlorinated water

Mix all the ingredients and store in a covered container at 75°F/20°C or warmer for 24 hours.

DAY 2:

10 oz/280 g flour/rye flour mixture

8 oz/230 g white bread flour

10 oz/280 ml distilled or dechlorinated water

There will be minimal, if any, activity at this point. Mix all the ingredients and cover. Keep at 75°F/20°C or warmer for 24 hours.

DAY 3:

10 oz/300 g sourdough culture

8 oz/230 g white bread flour

10 oz/280 ml distilled or dechlorinated water

You should start to notice small bubbles and/or foam forming at this point—you can now call it a (very weak) sourdough culture! If that is not happening, make sure your mixture is warm enough. It will not smell particularly nice at this point. Mix all ingredients and cover. Keep at 75°F/20°C or warmer for 24 hours.

DAY 4:

10 oz/300 g liquid sourdough

8 oz/230 g white bread flour

10 oz/280 ml distilled or dechlorinated water

Development should be continuing, with slightly larger bubbles forming as well as foam. Small amounts of liquid may form at the top of the mixture, which is normal. You should begin feeding two times per day at this point.

Mix all ingredients and cover. Keep at 75°F/20°C or warmer for 12 hours.

Continue this 12-hour feeding schedule for at least 3 days. After one full week from your first mixture, your sourdough culture should be strong enough to begin maintenance feedings, which will contain a lower percentage of sourdough culture. You can also start using your regular tap water at this point:

2 oz/40 ml liquid sourdough

8 oz/230 g white bread flour

10 oz/280 ml 75°F/20°C tap water

Once you have a healthy, vibrant starter chugging away, you can do one of two things. First, you can keep it on your counter and feed it every day. You can certainly get away with once-a-day feedings if you reduce your starter amount by half. If you plan correctly and know when your next bake is going to be, just switch back to your 12-hour feedings a couple of days before the big day so it can gain some momentum.

Or, if you know you're not going to be baking for a while, or you're going out of town, or you started one of those fad diets that tells you that the staple of civilization is suddenly going to kill you, just give it a feeding and pop it in the refrigerator. When you know your next baking day, or you come to your senses re: the fad diet thing, pull the starter out. Give it 12 hours to warm up, and then give it at least 2 days of 12-hour feedings to get the yeast and bacteria back on track.

Whether you're warming your starter up from hibernation in the fridge or just keeping it going on your counter, once your starter is nice and strong, you'll "build" to your mix. That is, 12 hours before the mix, you'll make a batch of starter sized for two things: enough to fulfill the needs of the recipe, and some extra to carry on the starter until the next batch. If you're building a different style of sourdough starter, say, a stiff starter with rye flour called a levain, you'll still carry on that liquid starter in a separate container. For example, if you're making Pain au Levain, 12 hours before the bake you'll use a small amount of liquid to make the stiffer levain starter. At the same time, you'll take another portion of the liquid and use that to carry your starter into the future, be it in cold storage or at room temperature. To simplify, just make sure you always have a bit of liquid starter left over to keep for your next batch of bread. Carry on the life cycle! It's the Baby Bee—or whatever you decide to call it.

NORTH SHORE SOURDOUGH
THE "WHEREVER-YOU-ARE" SOURDOUGH

This is the most basic sourdough we make at the bakery. We make it right from the Liquid Sourdough Starter, flake it with some whole wheat to give it a bit of color and texture and bake it to a beautifully dark golden brown. We call ours the North Shore Sourdough because of the culture's propensity toward adapting itself to the natural bacteria in a particular location. That's a major part of what gives sourdoughs their distinctive flavors. So, wherever you are, develop your culture, bake this bread and call it your own.

OVERVIEW

- Yield: Two 1 lb 12 oz/800-g loaves
- Desired Dough Temperature: 85°F/30°C
- Mixing Time: 40 minutes
- Bulk Fermentation: ~3 hours
- Proofing Time: ~2 hours
- Baking Time: ~25 minutes
- Cooling Time: ~3 hours

12 HOURS BEFORE THE BAKE

Mix your final starter. This will be enough for the bread formula, plus some extra to carry on the starter.

12.5 oz/350 ml 75°F/20°C water

2.5 oz/65 g liquid sourdough

10 oz/280 g white bread flour

BAKING DAY

1 lb 5.5 oz/640 g white bread flour

3.25 oz/90 g whole wheat flour

1 lb 6.5 oz/630 g liquid sourdough

13.25 oz/375 ml 95°F/35°C water

2 tsp/14 g fine sea salt

Combine both flours into your large mixing bowl. Pour your sourdough and water into another large bowl, and remember to keep that water warm to give your wild yeast a comfortable atmosphere to grow. Then, dump your flours on top of the liquid ingredients, and mix it by hand for about 30 seconds, until it comes together in a shaggy mass. Don't forget to scrape the bottom and sides of the bowl regularly; you want all of that flour hydrated and don't want to see any dry spots. Set aside in a warm place, at least 80°F/25°C, for 30 minutes. If you're having trouble finding your warm place, it's time to use your trusty heat lamp.

Sprinkle the salt on top of the dough, and grab a four-finger pinch of the dough and pull. It should stretch out like chunky taffy rather than just tear off. Incorporate the salt into the dough, continuously pushing the sides of the dough into the middle while turning the bowl. After a minute of this, the dough should be pulling away from the sides of the bowl and developing a bit of a sheen, and you shouldn't feel any crunchy salt crystals. Cover the bowl, and put it in your warm place for 30 minutes.

Turn your dough out onto a lightly floured surface and give it your four-fold (see page 35). It should make a tight little package—this is how we're building the dough's strength, and after every fold the dough's volume should increase. It should consistently feel warm and active. Roll the dough over and place it, seam side down, back into the bowl. Repeat this four-fold procedure every 30 minutes for the first 2 hours (you'll fold the dough four times in total), until the dough is strong but puffy, warm to the touch and holds a fingerprint when pressed into the surface. Leave the dough to gain some volume for the last hour. The whole process will take about 3 hours.

Once your dough is ready to cut, turn it out onto a floured work surface. Using your bench knife and scale, divide into two 1 pound 12 ounce/800-g pieces. Gently shape the dough into rounds (see page 38), being careful not to compress the dough too much, and place seam side down on your work surface. Cover and let rest for 20 minutes to build a bit more strength into the loaf before final shaping. This is what bakers call a "bench rest."

Dust two round bannetons lightly with flour; then take your rested rounds and gently but firmly shape them into rounds again. If your seams feel like they're coming undone when you lift a loaf up, give it a few minutes sitting seam side down on the table to seal it, and next time, use less flour for shaping. The dough's moisture should be enough to seal the loaf closed. Place your shaped loaves seam side up in your bannetons, cover with a cloth or plastic wrap and place in your trusty warm spot.

While your dough is proofing, place your baking stone on the lowest rack in your oven, and your cast-iron pan on the highest rack. Preheat your oven to 450°F/230°C. Check in on your bread periodically; if the surface feels dried out, spray it with a bit of water to allow for maximum expansion. If it feels cold, make it warmer. This proofing may take up to 2 hours, depending on the conditions of your kitchen. The loaf is ready to go in when it feels very airy and holds a fingerprint when pressed into the surface.

Flip the loaves over onto your peel. It might take a couple of batches to bake all your bread, depending on your oven size. Score the face of each loaf with your razor in your desired pattern. Now, grab three ice cubes from the freezer. Being careful to not keep the oven door open too long and let the heat out, open the oven, slide your loaves onto the stone, throw the three ice cubes into the cast-iron pan and close the door. After 5 minutes, quickly open the door and spray the interior of the oven with water. Continue baking until the loaves are evenly browned and have a nice hollow thump when you tap them on the bottom, about 25 minutes. Let cool for at least 3 hours before cutting.

POACHED GARLIC SOURDOUGH AND TOASTED WALNUT SOURDOUGH

THE TWINS

This is two breads in one—choose garlic or toasted walnuts for your addition. We love the aromatic garlic bread, and here's the key to it: We roast our garlic to the point where you could spread it on a cracker, and then fold it gently into the dough. The walnut bread uses the same dough, except that we fold in nuts rather than garlic. The walnuts have a curious reaction with the dough, turning it pale purple as the dough progresses. This one is equally at home spread with fresh chèvre as it is used in a fantastic French toast.

OVERVIEW

- Yield: Three 1 lb 8 oz/700-g loaves
- Desired Dough Temperature: 85°F/30°C
- Mixing Time: 40 minutes
- Bulk Fermentation: ~3 hours
- Proofing Time: ~2 hours
- Baking Time: ~25 minutes
- Cooling Time: ~3 hours

12 HOURS BEFORE THE BAKE

Mix your final starter. This will be enough for the bread formula, plus some extra to carry on the starter.

15 oz/445 ml 75°F/20°C water

3 oz/60 ml liquid sourdough

12 oz/340 g white bread flour

Prepare poached garlic or toasted walnuts (page 55)

BAKING DAY

1 lb 9.5 oz/720 g white bread flour

4 oz/110 g whole wheat flour

1 lb 7.75 oz/665 g liquid starter

1 lb 1 oz/480 ml 95°F/35°C water

3 ½ tsp/24 g fine sea salt

2.25 oz/65 g poached garlic, or 10.75 oz/305 g toasted walnuts

Combine both flours into your large mixing bowl. In another bowl, mix your liquid starter and water, and remember to keep that water warm to give your wild yeast a comfortable atmosphere to grow. Dump the flours on top of the liquid ingredients, and mix it by hand for about 30 seconds, until it comes together in a shaggy mass. Don't forget to scrape the bottom and sides of the bowl regularly; you want all of that flour hydrated and don't want to see any dry spots. Set aside in a warm place, at least 80°F/25°C, for 30 minutes.

Sprinkle the salt on top of the dough and grab a four-finger pinch of the dough and pull. It should stretch out like chunky taffy rather than just tear off. Incorporate the salt into the dough, continuously pushing the sides of the dough into the middle while turning the bowl. After a minute of this, the dough should be pulling away from the sides of the bowl and developing a bit of a sheen, and you shouldn't feel any crunchy salt crystals. Cover the bowl, and put it in your warm place for 30 minutes.

For Poached Garlic Sourdough. Toss the garlic into the bowl, and very gently incorporate into the mix. You'll want to crush some, but not all, of the cloves. Carefully push them into the dough while folding it over, but remember that your future folds will distribute the garlic evenly over the next couple of hours. Cover the bowl, and put it in your warm place for 30 minutes.

For Toasted Walnut Sourdough. Toss in the walnuts, and push them into the dough while folding it over, but remember that your future folds will distribute the walnuts evenly over the next couple of hours. Cover the bowl, and put it in your warm place for 30 minutes.

Turn your dough onto a lightly floured surface and give it your four-fold (see page 35). It should make a tight little package—and after every fold, the dough's volume should increase. It should consistently feel warm and active. Roll the dough over and place it, seam side down, back into the bowl. Repeat the four-fold procedure every 30 minutes for the first 2 hours (you'll fold the dough four times in total) until the dough is strong but puffy, warm to the touch and holds a fingerprint when pressed into the surface.

Leave the dough to gain some volume for the last hour. The whole process will take about 3 hours.

Once your dough is ready to cut, turn it onto a floured work surface. Using your bench knife and scale, divide into three 1 pound 8 ounce/700-g pieces. (If you're making the Toasted Walnut Sourdough, you'll have some extra dough at this point because of the added weight of the walnuts. Just distribute this dough equally among the three loaves.) Gently shape the dough into rounds (see page 38), being careful not to compress the dough too much, and place seam side down on your work surface. Cover and let rest for 20 minutes.

Next, dust three round bannetons lightly with flour and set them to the side. Take your rested rounds and gently but firmly shape them into rounds again. If the seams feel like they're coming undone when you lift a loaf up, give it a few minutes sitting seam side down on the table to seal it, and next time, use less flour for shaping. The dough's moisture should be enough to seal the loaf closed. Place your shaped loaves seam side up in the bannetons, cover with a cloth or plastic wrap and place in your trusty warm spot.

While your dough is proofing, place your baking stone on the lowest rack in your oven, and your cast-iron pan on the highest rack. Preheat the oven to 450°F/230°C. Check in on your bread periodically; if the surface feels dried out, spray it with a bit of water to allow for maximum expansion. If it feels cold, make it warmer. This may take up to 2 hours, depending on the conditions of your kitchen. The loaf is ready to go in when it feels very airy and holds a fingerprint when pressed into the surface.

Flip the loaves over onto your peel. It might take a couple of batches to bake all your bread, depending on your oven size. Score the face of each loaf with your razor in your desired pattern. Now, grab three ice cubes from the freezer. Being careful not to keep the oven door open too long and let the heat out, open the oven, slide your loaves onto the stone, throw the three ice cubes into the cast-iron pan and close the door. After 5 minutes, quickly open the door and spray the interior of the oven with water. Continue baking until the loaves are evenly browned, about 25 minutes, and have a nice hollow thump when you tap it on the bottom. Let cool for at least 3 hours before cutting.

POACHED GARLIC

1 cup/160 g garlic cloves, peeled

Canola oil to cover

Preheat the oven to 350°F/180°C. Place the cloves in a heavy-bottom saucepan and cover with the canola oil. Roast until they are very, very soft, about 1 hour.

Strain the oil out and let the garlic cool before using. The oil can be used for salad dressings, sautéing or anything else that might be enhanced by garlic-flavored oil.

TOASTED WALNUTS

10.75 oz/300 g walnut pieces

Preheat the oven to 375°F/190°C. Spread the walnut pieces on a sheet pan and toast for 10 minutes or until crispy and fragrant.

PAIN AU LEVAIN

THE SOURDOUGH LOVER'S SOURDOUGH

If there is a "most French" French bread that we bake here, the Pain au Levain is it. The translation of its name is "bread made from sourdough starter," and we call it the "baker's bread" because cooks in the know tend to be drawn to it. We make a 1 ¼-pound/550-g batard and a hefty 3-pound/1.5-kg round at the bakery; you can make an even bigger 5-pound/2-kg loaf from this recipe, provided you have the banneton and oven space to contain it. Making this bread takes an extra step than the North Shore Sourdough, as we're using the Liquid Sourdough Starter to make a rye-laden stiff starter—the Levain. So, give yourself an extra 12 hours for this one.

OVERVIEW

- Yield: Four 1 lb 4 oz/550-g loaves or one large, 5-lb/2-kg loaf
- Desired Dough Temperature: 85°F/30°C
- Mixing Time: 40 minutes
- Bulk Fermentation: ~3 hours
- Proofing Time: ~2 hours
- Baking Time: ~25 minutes
- Cooling Time: ~3 hours

12 HOURS BEFORE THE BAKE

Mix your levain (see page 47). This will be enough for the bread formula, plus some extra to carry on the starter.

5.75 oz/160 ml 75°F/20°C water

2 oz/40 ml liquid sourdough

9.5 oz/270 g white bread flour

0.75 oz/20 g whole rye flour

BAKING DAY

1 lb 15.25 oz/885 g white bread flour

2.25 oz/60 g whole wheat flour

1.5 oz/40 g whole rye flour

1 lb 1.5 oz/500 g levain

1 lb 10.5 oz/750 ml 95°F/35°C water

3 ¾ tsp/26 g fine sea salt

Combine all three flours into your large mixing bowl. In another bowl, combine your levain and water, and remember to keep that water warm to give your wild yeast a comfortable atmosphere to grow. (You should pull your levain apart with your fingers when adding it to the water, so it incorporates into the rest of the ingredients more easily.) Then, dump the flours on top of the liquid ingredients, and mix it by hand for about 30 seconds, until it comes together in a shaggy mass. Don't forget to scrape the bottom and sides of the bowl regularly; you want all of that flour hydrated and don't want to see any dry spots. Set aside in a warm place, at least 80°F/25°C, for 30 minutes. If you're having trouble finding your warm place, it's time to use your trusty heat lamp.

Sprinkle the salt on top of the dough and grab a four-finger pinch of the dough and pull. It should stretch out like chunky taffy rather than just tear off. Incorporate the salt into the dough, continuously pushing the sides of the dough into the middle while turning the bowl. After a minute of this, the dough should be pulling away from the sides of the bowl and developing a bit of a sheen, and you shouldn't feel any crunchy salt crystals. Cover the bowl, and put it in your warm place for 30 minutes.

Turn your dough onto a lightly floured surface and give it your four-fold (see page 35). It should make a tight little package—and after every fold the dough's volume should increase. It should consistently feel warm and active. Roll the dough over and place it, seam side down, back into the bowl. Repeat every 30 minutes for the first 2 hours (you'll fold the dough four times in total) until the dough is strong but puffy, warm to the touch and holds a fingerprint when pressed into the surface. Leave the dough to gain some volume for the last hour. The whole process will take about 3 hours.

Once your dough is ready to cut, turn it out onto a floured work surface. Using your bench knife and scale, divide into four 1 pound 4 ounce/550-g pieces (or keep as one large, 5 pound/2-kg loaf). Gently shape the dough into rounds (see page 38), being careful not to compress the dough too much, and place seam side down on your work surface. Cover and rest for 20 minutes to build a bit more strength into the loaf before final shaping. Set up your proofing board and couche to receive shaped breads (see page 20). If you're going with the large loaf, grab the biggest banneton you have, as it's going to take up a lot of room.

Take your rested rounds and gently but firmly shape them into tapered batards (see page 39), pinching the seams shut if necessary. Place your shaped loaves seam side up on the proofing board, couche them snugly and place in your trusty warm spot. (Alternatively, shape your 5 pound/2-kg loaf into a large round, and place seam side up in your mega banneton.)

While your dough is proofing, place your baking stone on the lowest rack in your oven, and your cast-iron pan on the highest rack. Preheat the oven to 450°F/230°C. Check in on your bread periodically; if the surface feels dried out, spray it with a bit of water to allow for maximum expansion. If it feels cold, make it warmer. This may take up to 2 hours, depending on the conditions of your kitchen. The loaf is ready to go in when it feels very airy and holds a fingerprint when pressed into the surface.

Flip the loaves over onto your peel. It might take a couple of batches to bake all your bread, depending on your oven size. Score each batard with two angled, overlapping slashes (or carve something nice into the face of your large, 5 pound/2-kg loaf). Now, grab three ice cubes from the freezer. Being careful to not keep the oven door open too long and let the heat out, open the oven, slide your loaf onto the stone, throw the three ice cubes into the cast-iron pan and close the door. After 5 minutes, quickly open the door and spray the interior of the oven with water. Continue baking until the loaves are evenly browned, about 25 minutes, and have a nice hollow thump when you tap them on the bottom. (A 5 pound/2-kg loaf might take upward of 45 minutes to bake all the way through, and may end up with a beautiful, super-dark crust. Embrace the dark side.) Let cool for at least 3 hours before cutting.

VARIATION: SOURDOUGH BAGUETTES

These can be made successfully with either the North Shore Sourdough or the Pain au Levain dough. There's one small trick that helps these baguettes burst better: Before you throw them in the oven, let them cool for about 30 minutes, either outdoors (if it's cold) or in your refrigerator. The drop in temperature followed by the quick heat of the oven gives an extra kick to the oven spring.

3 lb/1.5 kg sourdough dough, divided into four 12-oz/350-g pieces and preshaped into cylinders

While your dough is resting, set up your couche to receive baguettes and sprinkle it with a very thin layer of flour.

After 20 minutes of resting, shape each piece into 15-inch/38-cm tapered baguettes and loosely pleat (see page 40).

After about 45 minutes of resting, or just before you feel like the baguettes are ready to bake, place them in a very cool place for another 30 minutes. Score with three horizontal slashes, and load into the oven (using your standard three-ice-cube procedure), making sure they're well spaced. Two at a time is fine; just leave the other two in your cool spot until you're ready to bake them. They will take 20 to 25 minutes, or until they have a dark, golden crust. Let cool for 1 hour before cutting.

MARINATED OLIVE SOURDOUGH
BLACK AND GREEN, LIVING TOGETHER

This recipe is very similar to the Pain au Levain, with the added bonus of marinated olives. At the bakery, our olive loaf is our most popular sourdough, and it's easy to see why: Big chunks of salty olives pair with the tang of our longest-fermented bread, and it's bold, bold, bold. We actually have to reduce the salt percentage in this dough to make way for the briny ingredients. You can simply use rinsed black and green olives (pitted, please!), or you can marinate them for a few days to boost the flavor. Either way, if your green olives are very large, give them a few whacks with the chef's knife to break them up and allow them to incorporate into the dough a little more easily.

OVERVIEW

- Yield: Four 1 lb 4 oz/550-g loaves
- Desired Dough Temperature: 85°F/30°C
- Mixing Time: 40 minutes
- Bulk Fermentation: ~3 hours
- Proofing Time: ~2 hours
- Baking Time: ~25 minutes
- Cooling Time: ~3 hours

12 HOURS BEFORE THE BAKE

Mix your levain (see page 47). This will be enough for the bread formula, plus some extra to carry on the starter.

5.75 oz/160 ml 75°F/20°C water

2 oz/40 ml liquid sourdough

9.5 oz/270 g white bread flour

0.75 oz/20 g whole rye flour

Marinate olives (page 62)

BAKING DAY

1 lb 12 oz/790 g white bread flour

2 oz/60 g whole wheat flour

1.5 oz/40 g whole rye flour

14 oz/400 g levain

1 lb 10 oz/740 ml 95°F/35°C water

2 ½ tsp/17 g fine sea salt

8 oz/230 g marinated olives

Combine all three flours into your large mixing bowl. In another bowl, mix your levain and water, and remember to keep that water warm to give your wild yeast a comfortable atmosphere to grow. (You should pull your levain apart with your fingers when adding it to the water, so it incorporates into the rest of the ingredients more easily.) Then, dump the flours on top of the liquid ingredients, and mix by hand for about 30 seconds, until it comes together in a shaggy mass. Don't forget to scrape the bottom and sides of the bowl regularly; you want all of that flour hydrated and don't want to see any dry spots. Set aside in a warm place, at least 80°F/25°C, for 30 minutes. If you're having trouble finding your warm place, it's time to use your trusty heat lamp.

Sprinkle the salt on top of the dough and grab a four-finger pinch of the dough and pull. It should stretch out like chunky taffy rather than just tear off. Incorporate the salt into the dough, continuously pushing the sides of the dough into the middle while turning the bowl. After a minute of this, the dough should be pulling away from the sides of the bowl and developing a bit of a sheen, and you shouldn't feel any crunchy salt crystals. Dump your olives into the dough, and continue to incorporate. If you're using marinated olives, the oils will make incorporation a little more work. But remember, the folds will finish distributing the garnish into the dough, so don't sweat getting them all mixed in at this point. Cover the bowl, and put it in your warm place for 30 minutes.

Turn your dough onto a lightly floured surface and give it your four-fold (see page 35). It should make a tight little package and after every fold, the dough's volume should increase. It should consistently feel warm and active. Roll the dough over and place it, seam side down, back into the bowl. Repeat every 30 minutes for the first 2 hours (you'll fold the dough four times in total), until the dough is strong but puffy, warm to the touch and holds a fingerprint when pressed into the surface. Leave the dough to gain some volume for the last hour. The whole process will take about 3 hours.

Once your dough is ready to cut, turn it out onto your floured work surface. Using your bench knife and scale, divide into four 1 pound 4 ounce/550-g pieces. Gently shape the dough into rounds, being careful not to compress the dough too much, and place seam side down on your work surface. Cover and rest for 20 minutes to build a bit more strength into the loaf before the final shaping.

Next, take your rested rounds and gently but firmly shape them into stubby batards (see page 39), pinching the seams shut if necessary. Place your shaped loaves seam side up in the bannetons, cover them with a damp cloth or plastic wrap and put back in your warm place.

While your dough is proofing, place your baking stone on the lowest rack in your oven, and your cast-iron pan on the highest rack. Preheat the oven to 450°F/230°C. Check in on your bread periodically; if the surface feels dried out, spray it with a bit of water to allow for maximum expansion. If it feels cold, make it warmer. This may take up to 2 hours, depending on the conditions of your kitchen. The loaf is ready to go in when it feels very airy and holds a fingerprint when pressed into the surface.

Flip the loaves over onto your peel. It might take a couple of batches to bake all your bread, depending on your oven size. Score each batard with one long, angled slash, or with whichever design you prefer. Now, grab three ice cubes from the freezer. Being careful to not keep the oven door open too long and let the heat out, open the oven, slide your loaf onto the stone, throw the three ice cubes into the cast-iron pan and close the door. After 5 minutes, quickly open the door and spray the interior of the oven with water. Continue baking until the loaf is evenly browned, about 25 minutes, and has a nice hollow thump when you tap it on the bottom. Let cool for at least 3 hours before cutting.

MARINATED OLIVES

You can add whichever aromatics and spices you like to your olives. Citrus zest, cilantro, rosemary and crushed red pepper are popular options. Make this at least a day ahead of starting the bread.

8 oz/230 g mixed Sicilian and kalamata olives, pitted

½ cup/120 ml extra-virgin olive oil

2 tbsp/30 ml lemon juice

2 cloves garlic, minced

Pinch of dried basil

Pinch of dried oregano

Combine all of the ingredients in a small saucepan, and cook over low heat for 30 minutes. Cool completely before using.

BROWN ALE AND BARLEY BREAD
A FEW OF MY FAVORITE THINGS

It stands to reason that people obsessed with the fermentation of dough would be interested in fermentation of other things. Wine and beer come to mind immediately, especially as I am drinking a glass of homemade wine as I write this. But beer is applied to bread a little more traditionally. We like to use a darker ale in bread mixes, as a lager's lighter flavor profile will get lost in the dough, and hoppier brews add too much bitterness. Brown ale, or even stout, is best for this bread. Make sure to pour the beer into a bowl a few hours before you mix, to let it get flat, and make sure to warm it. It makes up the bulk of your hydration.

OVERVIEW

- Yield: Three 1 lb 10 oz/750-g loaves
- Desired Dough Temperature: 85°F/30°C
- Mixing Time: 40 minutes
- Bulk Fermentation: ~3 hours
- Proofing Time: ~2 hours
- Baking Time: ~25 minutes
- Cooling Time: ~3 hours

12 HOURS BEFORE THE BAKE

Mix your final starter (see page 63). This will be enough for the bread formula, plus some extra to carry on the starter.

16.25 oz/460 ml 75°F/20°C water

2.75 oz/50 ml liquid sourdough

13 oz/370 g white bread flour

BAKING DAY

2 lbs 2 oz/1 g white bread flour

4 oz/110 g whole wheat flour

1 oz/30 g whole rye flour

1 lb 11.25 oz/520 ml liquid sourdough

5.25 oz/150 ml 95°F/35°C water

1 lb 2 oz/510 ml quality brown ale (flat, warmed to 95°F/35°C)

4 ¾ tsp/33 g fine sea salt

7.75 oz/210 g pearled barley, soaked overnight and well-drained (presoaking weight)

Combine all three flours into your large mixing bowl. In another bowl, mix the liquid sourdough, water and ale, and remember to keep that water and beer warm to give your wild yeast a comfortable atmosphere to grow. Then, dump the flours on top of the liquid ingredients, and mix by hand for about 30 seconds, until it comes together in a shaggy mass. Don't forget to scrape the bottom and sides of the bowl regularly; you want all of that flour hydrated and don't want to see any dry spots. Set aside in a warm place, at least 80°F/25°C, for 30 minutes. If you're having trouble finding your warm place, it's time to use your trusty heat lamp.

Sprinkle the salt on top of the dough and grab a four-finger pinch of the dough and pull. It should stretch out like chunky taffy rather than just tear off. Incorporate the salt into the dough, continuously pushing the sides of the dough into the middle while turning the bowl. After a minute of this, the dough should be pulling away from the sides of the bowl and developing a bit of a sheen, and you shouldn't feel any crunchy salt crystals. Throw in the pearled barley, and continue to incorporate by hand. Remember, the fold will help distribute, so don't wear yourself out trying to mix it in perfectly. Cover the bowl, and put it in your warm place for 30 minutes.

Turn your dough onto a lightly floured surface and give it your four-fold (see page 35). It should make a tight little package, and after every fold, the dough's volume should increase. It should consistently feel warm and active. Roll the dough over and place it, seam side down, back into the bowl. Repeat every 30 minutes for the first 2 hours (you'll fold the dough four times in total) until the dough is strong but puffy, warm to the touch and holds a fingerprint when pressed into the surface. Leave the dough to gain some volume for the last hour. The whole process will take about 3 hours.

Once your dough is ready to cut, turn it out onto your floured work surface. Using your bench knife and scale, divide into three 1 pound 10 ounce/750-g pieces. Gently shape the dough into rounds (see page 38), being careful not to compress the dough too much, and place seam side down on your work surface. Cover and rest for 1 hour. Dust three bannetons with flour and set aside.

For this particular style, the fendu (see page 39), we call the next step "pinning" rather than "shaping," because, well, that's what it is. Dust your work surface with a good amount of flour, and gently scoop your rounded loaves up with your bench knife and place—still seam side down—on the flour.

Sprinkle some flour on the top of the loaf as well. Grab the thinnest rolling pin you have, such as a French one or a 1-inch/2.5-cm-diameter wooden dowel, and press down in the middle of the loaf. Roll the pin back and forth a bit, not pressing so hard that you actually cut through the dough, and then remove the pin to reveal a bisected loaf. Roll the two sides together, gently flip the loaf over and place in the banneton. Place the finished loaves in your warm place and cover with a towel.

While your dough is proofing, place your baking stone on the lowest rack in your oven and your cast-iron pan on the highest rack. Preheat the oven to 450°F/230°C. Check in on your bread periodically; if the surface feels dried out, spray it with a bit of water to allow for maximum expansion. If it feels cold, make it warmer. This may take up to 2 hours, depending on the conditions of your kitchen. The loaf is ready to go in when it feels very airy and holds a fingerprint when pressed into the surface.

Flip the loaves over onto your peel. It might take a couple of batches to bake all your bread, depending on your oven size. Now, grab three ice cubes from the freezer. Being careful to not keep the oven door open too long and let the heat out, open the oven, slide your loaf onto the stone, throw the three ice cubes into the cast-iron pan and close the door. After 5 minutes, quickly open the door and spray the interior of the oven with water. Continue baking until the loaf is evenly browned, about 25 minutes, and has a nice hollow thump when you tap it on the bottom. Let cool for at least 3 hours before cutting.

ASIAGO-CHILI BREAD
SMOKING DOUGH

Baker Jess L. (we have a couple of Jesses) pitches practically an idea a week for a new product, and Andy usually has a loaf sitting on his desk when he comes back from the weekend. They're all good, but this one caught his attention—it's not often one samples a bread that tastes like it's been slow-smoked. The cheese adds a nice richness to balance the spice, but you can tone down the heat by dropping the amount of granulated chipotle that goes into the formula. Keep the powdered chili at full power—you won't get the full effect without it.

OVERVIEW

- Yield: Three 1 lb 10 oz/750-g loaves
- Desired Dough Temperature: 85°F/30°C
- Mixing Time: 40 minutes
- Bulk Fermentation: ~2 hours
- Proofing Time: ~1.5 hours
- Baking Time: ~25 minutes
- Cooling Time: ~3 hours

12 HOURS BEFORE THE BAKE

Mix your final starter (see page 63). This will be enough for the bread formula, plus some extra to carry on the starter.

10 oz/280 ml 75°F/20°C water

2 oz/40 ml liquid sourdough

8 oz/230 g white bread flour

BAKING DAY

1 lb 5.5 oz/600 g bread flour

13.25 oz/375 g semolina flour

1 tsp/8 g granulated chipotle chili

1 tsp/8 g chipotle chili powder

7.25 oz/215 g liquid starter

1 lb 9 oz/710 ml 90°F/32°C water

1 oz/30 ml extra-virgin olive oil

4 tsp/28 g fine sea salt

1 tsp/4 g instant yeast

11.25 oz/320 g Asiago cheese, cut into small dice

Combine both flours and both versions of chipotle chili in your large mixing bowl. In another bowl, mix your liquid starter, water and oil, and remember to keep that water warm to give your wild yeast a comfortable atmosphere to grow. Then, dump the flours and spices on top of the liquid ingredients, and mix it by hand for about 30 seconds, until it comes together in a shaggy mass. Don't forget to scrape the bottom and sides of the bowl regularly; you want all of that flour hydrated and don't want to see any dry spots. Set aside in a warm place, at least 80°F/25°C, for 30 minutes. If you're having trouble finding your warm place, it's time to use your trusty heat lamp.

Sprinkle the salt and yeast on top of the dough and grab a four-finger pinch of the dough and pull. It should stretch out like chunky taffy rather than just tear off. Incorporate the salt into the dough, continuously pushing the sides of the dough into the middle while turning the bowl. After a minute of this, the dough should be pulling away from the sides of the bowl and developing a bit of a sheen, and you shouldn't feel any crunchy salt crystals. Throw in the diced cheese and continue mixing by hand until it's nicely incorporated. Remember, the folds will help distribute the cheese as well, so don't wear yourself out trying to mix it in perfectly. Cover the bowl, and put it in your warm place for 30 minutes.

Turn your dough onto a lightly floured surface and give it your four-fold (see page 35). It should make a tight little package and after every fold the dough's volume should increase. It should consistently feel warm and active. Roll the dough over and place it, seam side down, back into the bowl. Repeat every 30 minutes for the first 2 hours (you'll fold the dough four times in total) until the dough is strong but puffy, warm to the touch and holds a fingerprint when pressed into the surface. Leave the dough to gain some volume for the last hour. The whole process will take about 3 hours.

Once your dough is ready to cut, turn it out onto a floured work surface. Using your bench knife and scale, divide into three 1 pound 10 ounce/750-g pieces. Gently shape the dough into rounds (see page 38), being careful not to compress the dough too much, and place seam side down on your work surface. Cover and rest for 20 minutes to build a bit more strength into the loaf before final shaping.

Next, lightly dust three oval bannetons with semolina flour and set them to the side. Take your rested rounds and gently but firmly shape them into stubby batards (see page 39). Feel free to pinch the seam shut if it threatens to open after shaping. Place your shaped loaves seam side up in your bannetons, cover with a cloth or plastic wrap and place in your trusty warm spot.

While your dough is proofing, place your baking stone on the lowest rack in your oven, and your cast-iron pan on the highest rack. Preheat the oven to 450°F/230°C. Check in on your bread periodically; if the surface feels dried out, spray it with a bit of water to allow for maximum expansion. If it feels cold, make it warmer. This may take up to 2 hours, depending on the conditions of your kitchen. The loaf is ready to go in when it feels very airy and holds a fingerprint when pressed into the surface.

Flip the loaves over onto your peel. If you're worried about cheese on your baking stone, line your peel with pieces of parchment and load the bread onto that. It might take a couple of batches to bake all your bread, depending on your oven size. Score the face of the loaf with your razor in your desired pattern—we like to slash four or five "gills" down each side. Now, grab three ice cubes from the freezer. Being careful to not keep the oven door open too long and let the heat out, open the oven, slide your loaf onto the stone, throw the three ice cubes into the cast-iron pan and close the door. After 5 minutes, quickly open the door and spray the interior of the oven with water. Continue baking until the loaf is evenly browned, about 25 minutes, and has a nice hollow thump when you tap it on the bottom. Let cool for at least 1 hour before cutting.

CHEDDAR-CHIVE BREAD
CHEESE IT. CHEESE IT GOOD.

This is a fantastic bread for sandwiches, and we've had customers rave about using it for hamburger buns. The recipe below makes three larger boules—as our joy lies in ripping off hunks and swiping them across whatever's left on our plates—but you could also make the boules half-size and end up with six smaller rounds. Just keep an eye on smaller loaves in the oven, as they will take about 5 minutes less to bake.

OVERVIEW

- Yield: Three 1 lb 10 oz/750-g loaves
- Desired Dough Temperature: 85°F/30°C
- Mixing Time: 40 minutes
- Bulk Fermentation: ~2 hours
- Proofing Time: ~2.5 hours
- Baking Time: ~25 minutes
- Cooling Time: ~15 minutes

12 HOURS BEFORE THE BAKE

Mix your final starter (see page 63). This will be enough for the bread formula, plus some extra to carry on the starter.

8 oz/240 ml 75°F/20°C water

10 oz/280 g white bread flour

2 oz/40 ml liquid sourdough

BAKING DAY

2 lb 0.5 oz/1 kg white bread flour

4 oz/110 g corn flour

8 oz/230 g liquid starter

1 lb 5.5 oz/610 ml 90°F/32°C water

2 oz/60 ml extra-virgin olive oil

3 ¼ tsp/23 g fine sea salt

1 ¼ tsp/5 g instant yeast

10.5 oz/300 g sharp cheddar cheese, cut into small dice

1 small bunch chives, minced

Combine your flours into your large mixing bowl. In another bowl, mix your liquid starter, water and olive oil, and remember to keep that water warm to give your yeast a comfortable atmosphere to grow. Then, dump the flours on top of the liquid ingredients, and mix it by hand for about 30 seconds, until it comes together in a shaggy mass. Don't forget to scrape the bottom and sides of the bowl regularly; you want all of that flour hydrated and don't want to see any dry spots. Set aside in a warm place, at least 80°F/25°C, for 30 minutes. If you're having trouble finding your warm place, it's time to use your trusty heat lamp.

Sprinkle the salt and yeast on top of the dough and grab a four-finger pinch of the dough and pull. It should stretch out like chunky taffy rather than just tear off. Incorporate the salt and yeast into the dough, continuously pushing the sides of the dough into the middle while turning the bowl. After a minute of this, the dough should be pulling away from the sides of the bowl and developing a bit of a sheen, and you shouldn't feel any crunchy salt crystals. Mix in the cheese and chives using the same motion. Remember, they will keep getting mixed in with the folds, so don't wear yourself out getting them perfectly distributed. Cover the bowl, and put it in your warm place for 30 minutes.

Turn your dough onto a lightly floured surface and give it your four-fold (see page 35). It should make a tight little package and after every fold the dough's volume should increase. It should consistently feel warm and active. Roll the dough over and place it, seam side down, back into the bowl. Repeat every 30 minutes (you'll fold the dough three times in total) until the dough is strong but puffy, warm to the touch and holds a fingerprint when pressed into the surface. The whole process will take about 2 hours.

Once your dough is ready to cut, turn it out onto a floured work surface. Using your bench knife and scale, divide into three 1 pound 10 ounce/750-g pieces. Gently shape the dough into rounds (see page 38), being careful not to compress the dough too much, and place seam side down on your work surface. Cover and rest for 20 minutes to build a bit more strength into the loaf before final shaping. While you're waiting, dust three round bannetons with corn flour.

Then, take your rested rounds and gently but firmly shape them into rounds again. If your seams feel like they're coming undone when you lift the loaf up, give it a few minutes sitting seam side down on the table to seal it, and next time, use less flour for shaping. The dough's moisture should be enough to seal the loaf closed. Be careful not to shape them too tightly, or little cheese squares will continuously pop through the surface of the loaf. Place your shaped loaves seam side up in your bannetons, cover with a cloth or plastic wrap and place in your trusty warm spot.

While your dough is proofing, place your baking stone on the lowest rack in your oven, and your cast-iron pan on the highest rack. Preheat the oven to 450˚F/230°C. Check in on your bread periodically; if the surface feels dried out, spray it with a bit of water to allow for maximum expansion. If it feels cold, make it warmer. This may take up to an hour, depending on the conditions of your kitchen. The loaf is ready to go in when it feels very airy and holds a fingerprint when pressed into the surface.

Flip the loaves over onto your peel. It might take a couple of batches to bake all your bread, depending on your oven size. Score the face of the loaf with your razor in your desired pattern. Before you load your bread, lay a piece of parchment paper down on the baking stone to catch any cheese that melts out of your loaf; burning cheddar is not a pleasant smell. Now, grab three ice cubes from the freezer. Being careful to not keep the oven door open too long and let the heat out, open the oven, slide your loaf onto the parchment-lined stone, throw the three ice cubes into the cast-iron pan and close the door. After 5 minutes, quickly open the door and spray the interior of the oven with water. Continue baking until the loaf is evenly browned, about 25 minutes, and has a nice hollow thump when you tap it on the bottom. Let cool for at least 1 hour before cutting.

RYE-RAISIN-PECAN SOURDOUGH
NUTTY, GRASSY, SWEET AND SOUR

Nuts and dried fruit do particularly well paired with rye. There's something about the earthy, grassy nature of the grain that allows it to not be overpowered by other strong ingredients. This makes particularly good toast, spread with a layer of homemade jam or cream cheese. Have it with a cup of tea, and that's breakfast right there.

OVERVIEW
- Yield: Three 1 lb 10 oz/750-g loaves
- Desired Dough Temperature: 85°F/30°C
- Mixing Time: 40 minutes
- Bulk Fermentation: ~2 hours
- Proofing Time: ~2 hours
- Baking Time: ~25 minutes
- Cooling Time: ~1 hour

12 HOURS BEFORE THE BAKE
Mix your levain (see page 47). This will be enough for the bread formula, plus some extra to carry on the starter.

1 oz/30 ml 75°F/20°C water

2 oz/40 ml liquid sourdough

5 oz/140 g white bread flour

0.5 oz/14 g whole rye flour

BAKING DAY
1 lb 7 oz/650 g white bread flour

9 oz/250 g whole rye flour

8 oz/160 g levain

1 lb 7.75 oz/675 ml 90°F/32°C water

3 ½ tsp/25 g fine sea salt

1 ¼ tsp/5 g instant yeast

8 oz/250 g raisins, soaked in hot water for 20 minutes and well drained

7.5 oz/215 g small pecan pieces, toasted

Combine both flours in your large mixing bowl. In another bowl, mix your levain and water, and remember to keep that water warm to give your wild yeast a comfortable atmosphere to grow. (You should pull your levain apart with your fingers when adding it to the water, so it incorporates into the rest of the ingredients more easily.) Then, dump the flours on top of the liquid ingredients, and mix it by hand for about 30 seconds, until it comes together in a shaggy mass. Don't forget to scrape the bottom and sides of the bowl regularly; you want all of that flour hydrated and don't want to see any dry spots. Set aside in a warm place, at least 80°F/25°C, for 30 minutes. If you're having trouble finding your warm place, it's time to use your trusty heat lamp.

Sprinkle the salt and yeast on top of the dough and grab a four-finger pinch of the dough and pull. It should stretch out like chunky taffy rather than just tear off. Incorporate the salt and yeast into the dough, continuously pushing the sides of the dough into the middle while turning the bowl. After a minute of this, the dough should be pulling away from the sides of the bowl and developing a bit of a sheen, and you shouldn't feel any crunchy salt crystals. Toss in the raisins and pecans, and using the same mixing motion, incorporate them into the dough. Remember, your four folds will distribute everything evenly, so don't wear your arms out with this step. Cover the bowl, and put it in your warm place for 30 minutes.

Turn your dough onto a lightly floured surface and give it your four-fold (see page 35). It should make a tight little package and after every fold the dough's volume should increase. It should consistently feel warm and active. Roll the dough over and place it, seam side down, back into the bowl. Repeat every 30 minutes for the first 2 hours (you'll fold the dough three times in total), until the dough is strong but puffy, warm to the touch and holds a fingerprint when pressed into the surface. The whole process will take about 2 hours.

Once your dough is ready to cut, turn it out onto a floured work surface. Using your bench knife and scale, divide into three 1 pound 10 ounce/750-g pieces. Gently shape the dough into rounds (see page 38), being careful not to compress the dough too much, and place seam side down on your work surface. Cover and rest for 20 minutes to build a bit more strength into the loaf before final shaping.

Next, dust three round bannetons lightly with flour and set them to the side. Take your rested rounds and gently but firmly shape them into rounds again. If your seams feel like they're coming undone when you lift the loaf up, give it a few minutes sitting seam side down on the table to seal it, and next time, use less flour for shaping. The dough's moisture should be enough to seal the loaf closed. Place your shaped loaves seam side up in your bannetons, cover with a cloth or plastic wrap and place in your trusty warm spot.

While your dough is proofing, place your baking stone on the lowest rack in your oven, and your cast-iron pan on the highest rack. Preheat the oven to 425°F/220°C. Check in on your bread periodically; if the surface feels dried out, spray it with a bit of water to allow for maximum expansion. If it feels cold, make it warmer. This may take up to 3 hours, depending on the conditions of your kitchen. The loaf is ready to go in when it feels very airy and holds a fingerprint when pressed into the surface.

Flip the loaves over onto your peel. It might take a couple of batches to bake all your bread, depending on your oven size. Score the face of the loaf with your razor in your desired pattern. Now, grab three ice cubes from the freezer. Being careful to not keep the oven door open too long and let the heat out, open the oven, slide your loaf onto the stone, throw the three ice cubes into the cast-iron pan and close the door. After 5 minutes, quickly open the door and spray the interior of the oven with water. Continue baking until the loaf is evenly browned, about 25 minutes, and has a nice hollow thump when you tap it on the bottom. Let cool for at least 1 hour before cutting.

ENGLISH MUFFIN TOASTING BREAD
YE OLDE BAKESHOPPE BREADE

Oh boy, do we love this bread created by baker Sara P. (or as we call her, "the duck"). It's the one we love to bring home, toast up with homemade jams, snack on at the bakery and have on weekend mornings. We use three different leaveners in this bread: wild yeast from the liquid starter (for tang), commercial yeast (for a quick rise) and baking soda (for a uniformly open crumb). It's worth investing in a square-sided Pullman pan just for this bread, because it's so easy to make and will become a family favorite at your house, too. You'll need a bit of semolina flour to coat your pan and garnish the loaf.

OVERVIEW
- Yield: One 3-lb/1.5-kg Pullman loaf
- Desired Dough Temperature: 85°F/30°C
- Mixing Time: 40 minutes
- Proofing Time: 3+ hours
- Baking Time: 40+ minutes
- Cooling Time: 3+ hours

12 HOURS BEFORE THE BAKE
Mix your final starter (see page 63). This will be enough for the bread formula, plus some extra to carry on the starter.

10 oz/280 ml 75°F/20°C water

2 oz/40 ml liquid sourdough

8 oz/230 g white bread flour

BAKING DAY
1 lb 1.75 oz/500 g white bread flour

1.5 oz/40 g whole wheat flour

1.5 oz/45 g granulated sugar

¼ tsp/1 g baking soda

2 tsp/15 g fine sea salt

¾ tsp/3 g instant yeast

10.25 oz/290 g liquid starter

15.5 oz/440 ml 80°F/25°C water

1.5 oz/45 g milk powder

Semolina flour, for dusting

Combine your flours, sugar, baking soda, salt and yeast into your large mixing bowl. In another bowl, combine your liquid starter, water and milk powder, and remember to keep that water warm to give your yeast a comfortable atmosphere to grow. Then, dump your dry ingredients on top of the liquid ingredients, and mix it by hand for about 30 seconds, until it resembles a smooth batter. Don't forget to scrape the bottom of the bowl to make sure everything is incorporated—a whisk might work better than your hands after a certain point. Set aside in a warm place, at least 80°F/25°C, for 30 minutes. If you're having trouble finding your warm place, it's time to use your trusty heat lamp.

After an hour, you're going to fold your dough, but the process will look a lot different with this particular dough. We call it the "flop": Reach into

the bowl and, with two hands, scoop the top quarter of the batter and flop it toward the middle. Do this for the bottom, and then both sides, and then repeat the flop a second time. Cover the bowl and set aside in your warm place for another hour.

In the meantime, oil your Pullman pan, and coat the entire inside with semolina flour by scooping a cup into the pan and knocking it around a bit. Dump out the excess. Pour the batter into the pan, and spread it around a bit to even out the surface. Put the loaf back into your warm place for the final rise. If you have a deep plastic bin, cover the pan with that, as a cloth or plastic will stick to the surface as the dough rises. If not, just keep an eye out for the surface drying and spritz accordingly.

After 1 more hour, the batter will have risen to about ½ inch/1 cm from the surface of the pan. If it's not there yet, just hold on until it is. In the meantime, preheat your oven to 400°F/200°C and arrange the racks so that the pan can cook on the baking stone and not bump into the rack above. When your dough is finally ready, sprinkle the surface with a dusting of semolina flour and slide the pan directly onto the stone. Bake for about 40 minutes, or until the surface is dark brown and the sides and bottom are golden. Remove the loaf from the pan immediately and cool on its side; this prevents the sides from collapsing as the interior firms up. Let cool for at least 2 hours before cutting and toasting.

CRANBERRY-WALNUT BREAD
A LITTLE SWEET, A LITTLE NUTTY

Our very first PM baker, Jereme, came up with this formula, which mixes our liquid sourdough culture with commercial yeast. The goal was to put a little tang in the bread to counterbalance the sweetness of the turbinado sugar. The result is a loaf that is sweet and sour, like cranberries themselves, and goes to show that you can use your culture as an accent, rather than a centerpiece, with no less impressive results. It's a customer favorite. There's a little prep to do beforehand—toasting walnut pieces and grinding walnut meal—but it's not too bad. Try and get them done the day before so you're not flailing on baking day!

OVERVIEW

- Yield: Three 1 lb 8 oz/700-g loaves; or eighteen 4-oz/100-g rolls
- Desired Dough Temperature: 85°F/30°C
- Mixing Time: 40 minutes
- Bulk Fermentation: 3+ hours
- Proofing Time: 3+ hours
- Baking Time: 25+ minutes
- Cooling Time: 3+ hours

12 HOURS BEFORE THE BAKE

Mix your final starter (see page 63). This will be enough for the bread formula, plus some extra to carry on the starter.

10 oz/280 ml 75°F/20°C water

2 oz/40 ml liquid sourdough

8 oz/230 g white bread flour

BAKING DAY

1 lb 10.5 oz/750 g white bread flour

2.5 oz/65 g turbinado sugar

10.5 oz/300 g liquid starter

1 lb/450 ml 90°F/32°C water

2 ½ tsp/18 g fine sea salt

2 tsp/8 g instant yeast

7.5 oz/215 g toasted walnut pieces

3 oz/75 g raw ground walnut meal

5.5 oz/160 g dried cranberries

Combine your flour and sugar in your large mixing bowl. In another bowl, mix your liquid starter and water, and remember to keep that water warm to give your yeast a comfortable atmosphere to grow. Then, dump your flour and sugar on top of the liquid ingredients, and mix it by hand for about 30 seconds, until it comes together in a shaggy mass. Don't forget to scrape the bottom and sides of the bowl regularly; you want all of that flour hydrated and don't want to see any dry spots. Set aside in a warm place, at least 80°F/25°C, for 30 minutes. If you're having trouble finding your warm place, it's time to use your trusty heat lamp.

Sprinkle the salt and the yeast on top of the dough and grab a four-finger pinch of the dough and pull. It should stretch out like chunky taffy rather than just tear off. Incorporate the salt and yeast into the dough, continuously pushing the sides of the dough into the middle while turning the bowl. After a minute

of this, add in your walnuts, walnut meal and cranberries and continue that incorporating action until everything is evenly distributed. Cover the bowl, and put it in your warm place for 30 minutes.

Turn your dough onto a lightly floured surface and give it your four-fold (see page 35). It should make a tight little package and after every fold the dough's volume should increase. It should consistently feel warm and active. Roll the dough over and place it, seam side down, back into the bowl. Repeat every 30 minutes until the dough is strong but puffy, warm to the touch and holds a fingerprint when pressed into the surface. The whole process will take about 2 hours.

Once your dough is ready to cut, turn it out onto your floured work surface. Using your bench knife and scale, divide into three 1 pound 8 ounce/700-g pieces. Gently shape the dough into rounds (see page 38), being careful not to compress the dough too much, and place seam side down on your work surface. Cover and rest for 20 minutes to build a bit more strength into the loaf before final shaping. (Alternatively, you can divide the dough into 4 ounce/100-g pieces, roll into little rounds and place on a sheet pan for rolls.)

Next, dust three round bannetons lightly with flour and set them to the side. Take your rested rounds and gently but firmly shape them into rounds again. If your seams feel like they're coming undone when you lift the loaf up, give it a few minutes sitting seam side down on the table to seal it, and next time, use less flour for shaping. The dough's moisture should be enough to seal the loaf closed. Place your shaped loaves seam side up in your bannetons, cover with a cloth or plastic wrap and place in your trusty warm spot.

While your dough is proofing, place your baking stone on the lowest rack in your oven, and your cast-iron pan on the highest rack. Preheat the oven to 425°F/220°C. Check in on your bread periodically; if the surface feels dried out, spray it with a bit of water to allow for maximum expansion. If it feels cold, make it warmer. This may take up to 2 hours, depending on the conditions of your kitchen (or only an hour if making rolls). The loaf is ready to go in when it feels very airy and holds a fingerprint when pressed into the surface.

Flip the loaves over onto your peel. It might take a couple of batches to bake all your bread, depending on your oven size. Score the face of the loaf with your razor in your desired pattern. (If you're making rolls, slash a small cross into the surface of each one to allow for a bit of expansion.) Now, grab three ice cubes from the freezer. Being careful to not keep the oven door open too long and let the heat out, open the oven, slide your loaf onto the stone, throw the three ice cubes into the cast-iron pan and close the door. After 5 minutes, quickly open the door and spray the interior of the oven with water. Continue baking until the loaf is evenly browned, about 25 minutes (15 minutes for rolls), and has a nice hollow thump when you tap it on the bottom. Let cool for at least 30 minutes before cutting.

Toasted Walnuts: Place walnut pieces on a baking tray, and toast in a 375°F/190°C oven for 10 minutes or until crispy and fragrant.

Walnut Meal: Process raw walnuts in a food processor until they become a fine meal.

CARAWAY-RYE SOURDOUGH

GET YOUR DELI MEATS READY

There's almost no other sandwich Andy prefers more than a Reuben. Pastrami piled high with sauerkraut and Russian dressing (and seriously, he'll send it back if it doesn't have enough kraut or dressing) is his go-to sandwich. So, because a great rye loaf is essential to a good deli sandwich like this, it makes sense that we'd develop one. If only to serve Andy's singular purpose.

OVERVIEW

- Yield: Two 1 lb 10 oz/750-g 5-in × 9-in/12-cm × 23-cm pan loaves
- Desired Dough Temperature: 85°F/30°C
- Mixing Time: 40 minutes
- Bulk Fermentation: 1+ hours
- Proofing Time: 3+ hours
- Baking Time: 25+ minutes
- Cooling Time: 3+ hours

12 HOURS BEFORE THE BAKE

Mix your levain (see page 47). Remember to save some liquid starter to carry on the sourdough!

4 oz/115 ml 75°F/20°C water

1.25 oz/25 ml liquid sourdough

6.5 oz/180 g bread flour

0.5 oz/14 g whole rye flour

BAKING DAY

1 lb 3.5 oz/550 g white bread flour

4.25 oz/120 g whole rye flour

8.25 oz/230 g levain

1 lb 1.75 oz/500 ml 90°F/32°C water

2 ¼ tsp/16 g fine sea salt

1 tsp/4 g instant yeast

1 ½ tbsp/15 g caraway seeds

Combine your flours in your large mixing bowl. In another bowl, combine your levain and water, and remember to keep that water warm to give your wild yeast a comfortable atmosphere to grow. (You should pull your levain apart with your fingers when adding it to the water, so it incorporates into the rest of the ingredients more easily.) Then, dump the flours on top of the liquid ingredients, and mix it by hand for about 30 seconds, until it comes together in a shaggy mass. Don't forget to scrape the bottom and sides of the bowl regularly; you want all of that flour hydrated and don't want to see any dry spots. Set aside in a warm place, at least 80°F/25°C, for 30 minutes. If you're having trouble finding your warm place, it's time to use your trusty heat lamp.

Sprinkle the salt, yeast and caraway seeds on top of the dough and grab a four-finger pinch of the dough and pull. It should stretch out like chunky taffy rather than just tear off. Incorporate the salt and yeast into the dough, continuously pushing the sides of the dough into the middle while turning the bowl. Cover the bowl, and put it in your warm place for 30 minutes.

Turn your dough onto a lightly floured surface and give it your four-fold (see page 35). It should make a tight little package and after every fold the dough's volume should increase. It should consistently feel warm and active. Roll the dough over and place it, seam side down, back into the bowl. Repeat every 30 minutes until the dough is strong but puffy, warm to the touch and holds a fingerprint when pressed into the surface. This will take about 2 hours.

Once your dough is ready to cut, turn it out onto your floured work surface. Using your bench knife and scale, divide into two 1 pound 10 ounce/750-g pieces. Gently shape the dough into rounds (see page 38), being careful not to compress the dough too much, and place seam side down on your work surface. Cover and rest for 20 minutes to build a bit more strength into the loaf before final shaping.

Next, lightly oil your 5-inch × 9-inch/12 × 23-cm bread pans and set them to the side. Take your rested rounds and gently but firmly shape them into stubby cylinders (see page 39), leaving the first seam side down on the table as you shape the second. Place your shaped loaves seam side down in your loaf pans, cover with a damp cloth or plastic wrap and place in your trusty warm spot.

While your dough is proofing, place your baking stone on the lowest rack in your oven, and your cast-iron pan on the highest rack. Preheat the oven to 450°F/230°C. Check in on your bread periodically; if the surface feels dried out, spray it with a bit of water to allow for maximum expansion. If it feels cold, make it warmer. This may take up to 2 hours, depending on the conditions of your kitchen. The loaf is ready to go in when it feels very airy and holds a fingerprint when pressed into the surface.

When you're ready to bake, score the face of the loaf with four or five diagonal slashes. This releases tension in two directions, so when the oven spring occurs, you get a nice, even expansion of the surface of the loaf. Now, grab three ice cubes from the freezer. Being careful to not keep the oven door open too long and let the heat out, open the oven, slide your loaves onto the stone, throw the three ice cubes into the cast-iron pan and close the door. After 5 minutes, quickly open the door and spray the interior of the oven with water. Continue baking until the loaf is evenly browned, about 25 minutes, and has a nice hollow thump when you tap it on the bottom. Immediately, but carefully, remove the loaves from the pans and place them on a cooling rack. If the sides and bottom of the loaf look light, feel free to pop them back in the oven for a few minutes. Let cool for at least 3 hours before cutting.

100 PERCENT WHOLE WHEAT PAN LOAVES
THE HEALTHY ONE

This dough is one of the only ones we make at the bakery that is 100 percent whole grain. Dealing with breads that contain no white flour always poses the same problem: They have a propensity to come out dense and chewy and to have little to no oven burst. The little bits of bran and germ that make whole wheat flour so cleansing for your gut act like little knives that pierce the gluten matrix as the dough proofs. Our solution is to build strength in the existing gluten through a whole wheat poolish, which absorbs water overnight, and to add olive oil to lubricate the strands of developing gluten and allow for more stretching. The honey serves as a foil for the increased bitterness due to the whole grain and the olive oil, and also to add that bit of sweetness that makes for great toast, with or without butter.
We have it with!

OVERVIEW

- Yield: Two 2 lb/1 kg 5-in × 9-in/12-cm × 23-cm pan loaves
- Desired Dough Temperature: 85°F/30°C
- Mixing Time: 40 minutes
- Bulk Fermentation: ~2 hours
- Proofing Time: ~1.5 hours
- Baking Time: ~25 minutes
- Cooling Time: ~3 hours

12 HOURS BEFORE THE BAKE

Mix your whole wheat poolish (see page 27).

12.75 oz/360 ml 75°F/20°C water

½ tsp/2 g instant yeast

12 oz/340 g whole wheat flour

BAKING DAY

1 lb 7.5 oz/665 g whole wheat poolish

12.75 oz/360 ml 90°F/32°C water

2 oz/60 ml extra-virgin olive oil

1.5 oz/40 g honey

1 lb 7.75 oz/670 g whole wheat flour

3 tsp/20 g fine sea salt

¾ tsp/3 g instant yeast

½ cup/80 g sesame seeds (optional)

In a large bowl, combine the poolish, water, olive oil and honey, and remember to keep that water warm to give your wild yeast a comfortable atmosphere to grow. Swish the liquid ingredients around a bit to break up the honey. Then, dump your flour on top of the liquid ingredients, and mix it by hand for about 30 seconds, until it comes together in a shaggy mass. Don't forget to scrape the bottom and sides of the bowl regularly; you want all of that flour hydrated and don't want to see any dry spots. Set aside in a warm place, at least 80°F/25°C, for 30 minutes. If you're having trouble finding your warm place, it's time to use your trusty heat lamp.

Sprinkle the salt and yeast on top of the dough and grab a four-finger pinch of the dough and pull. It should stretch out like chunky taffy rather than just tear off. Incorporate the salt and yeast into the dough, continuously pushing the sides of the dough into the middle while turning the bowl. After a minute of this, the dough should be pulling away from the sides of the bowl and developing a bit of a sheen, and you shouldn't feel any crunchy salt crystals. Cover the bowl, and put it in your warm place for 30 minutes.

Turn your dough onto a lightly floured surface and give it your four-fold (see page 35). It should make a tight little package and after every fold the dough's volume should increase. It should consistently feel warm and active. Roll the dough over and place it, seam side down, back into the bowl. Repeat every 30 minutes (you'll fold the dough three times in total) until the dough is strong but puffy, warm to the touch and holds a fingerprint when pressed into the surface. The whole process will take about 2 hours.

Once your dough is ready to cut, turn it out onto your floured work surface. Using your bench knife and scale, divide into two 2 pound/1-kg pieces. Gently shape the dough into rounds (see page 39), being careful not to compress the dough too much, and place seam side down on your work surface. Cover and rest for 20 minutes to build a bit more strength into the loaf before final shaping.

Next, lightly oil two 5-inch × 9-inch/12 × 23-cm bread pans and set them to the side. Take your rested rounds and gently but firmly shape them into stubby cylinders (see page 39), leaving them seam side down on the table. If you like, you can spray the surface of each loaf with water and roll in the sesame seeds for a more interesting crust. Place your shaped loaves seam side down in your loaf pans, cover with a damp cloth or plastic wrap and place in your trusty warm spot.

While your dough is proofing, place your baking stone on the lowest rack in your oven, and your cast-iron pan on the highest rack. Preheat the oven to 450°F/230°C. Check in on your bread periodically; if the surface feels dried out, spray it with a bit of water to allow for maximum expansion. If it feels cold, make it warmer. This may take up to 2 hours, depending on the conditions of your kitchen. The loaf is ready to go in when it feels very airy and holds a fingerprint when pressed into the surface. This is a pretty dense loaf, so it will always feel a bit more solid than other bread you have worked with.

When you're ready to bake, score the face of the loaf with four or five diagonal slashes. This releases tension in two directions, so when the oven spring occurs, you get a nice, even expansion of the surface of the loaf. Now, grab three ice cubes from the freezer. Being careful to not keep the oven door open too long and let the heat out, open the oven, slide your loaves onto the stone, throw the three ice cubes into the cast-iron pan and close the door. After 5 minutes, quickly open the door and spray the interior of the oven with water. Continue baking until the loaf is evenly browned, about 30 minutes, and has a nice hollow thump when you tap it on the bottom. Immediately, but carefully, remove the loaves from the pans and place them on a cooling rack. If the sides and bottom of the loaf look light, feel free to pop them back in the oven for a few minutes. Let cool for at least 3 hours before cutting.

MULTIGRAIN BREAD
ENGLISH FOR "MULTIPLE GRAINS"

The combination of the toasted grains on the outside of this bread and the softer, slightly hydrated seeds on the interior give our multigrain a nice one-two punch. We're giving you our total seed mix amount here (we chose six different grains for this bread because five and seven grains are so passé!), but feel free to experiment with any grains and seeds you wish, as long as they're hulled or not too tough. If you're not sure, you can soak them in water for a few hours (up to overnight) to soften them a bit.

OVERVIEW
- Yield: Three 1 lb 10 oz/750-g loaves
- Desired Dough Temperature: 85°F/30°C
- Mixing Time: 40 minutes
- Bulk Fermentation: ~2 hours
- Proofing Time: ~1.5 hours
- Baking Time: ~25 minutes
- Cooling Time: ~3 hours

12 HOURS BEFORE THE BAKE
Mix your biga (see page 29).
8 oz/240 ml 75°F/20°C water
13 oz/370 g white bread flour
½ tsp/2 g instant yeast

BAKING DAY
1 lb 6.75 oz/640 g whole wheat flour
9.5 oz/270 g white bread flour
1 lb 5 oz/600 g biga
1 lb 10 oz/740 ml 90°F/32°C water
4 tsp/28 g fine sea salt
1 ¼ tsp/5 g instant yeast
1 lb/450 g seed mix (page 83)

Combine both flours in your large mixing bowl. In another bowl, combine your biga and water, and remember to keep that water warm to give your yeast a comfortable atmosphere to grow. (You should pull your biga apart with your fingers when adding it to the water, so it incorporates into the rest of the ingredients more easily.) Then, dump the flours on top of the liquid ingredients, and mix it by hand for about 30 seconds, until it comes together in a shaggy mass. Don't forget to scrape the bottom and sides of the bowl regularly; you want all of that flour hydrated and don't want to see any dry spots. Set aside in a warm place, at least 80°F/25°C, for 30 minutes. If you're having trouble finding your warm place, it's time to use your trusty heat lamp.

Sprinkle the salt and yeast on top of the dough and grab a four-finger pinch of the dough and pull. It should stretch out like chunky taffy rather than just tear off. Incorporate the salt and yeast into the dough, continuously pushing the sides of the dough into the middle while turning the bowl. After a minute of this, the dough should be pulling away from the sides of the bowl and developing a bit of a sheen, and you shouldn't feel any crunchy salt crystals. Pour in 12 ounces/350 g of your seed mix, and continue to incorporate until the seeds are spread throughout the dough. The folding process will make sure they're all

mixed in, so if your arm tires out, that's okay. Just get them halfway there. Cover the bowl, and put it in your warm place for 30 minutes.

Turn your dough onto a lightly floured surface and give it your four-fold (see page 35). It should make a tight little package and after every fold the dough's volume should increase. It should consistently feel warm and active. Roll the dough over and place it, seam side down, back into the bowl. Repeat every 30 minutes (you'll fold the dough three times in total) until the dough is strong but puffy, warm to the touch and holds a fingerprint when pressed into the surface. The whole process will take about 2 hours.

Once your dough is ready to cut, turn it out onto your floured work surface. Using your bench knife and scale, divide into three 1 pound 10 ounce/750-g pieces. Gently shape the dough into rounds (see page 38), being careful not to compress the dough too much, and place seam side down on your work surface. Cover and rest for 20 minutes to build a bit more strength into the loaf before final shaping.

Next, grab those three oval bannetons and set them to the side. Take your rested rounds and gently but firmly shape them into stubby batards (see page 39). If your seams feel like they're coming undone when you lift the loaf up, give it a few minutes sitting seam side down on the table to seal it, and next time, use less flour for shaping. The dough's moisture should be enough to seal the loaf closed. To garnish, spray the surface with water and roll the top of the shaped loaves on a plate containing the remaining 4 ounces/100 g of your seed mixture. Place your shaped loaves seam side up in your bannetons, cover with a cloth or plastic wrap and place in your trusty warm spot. If you do not have the fancy proofing baskets, you can actually rise these loaves seam side down right on a floured proofing board. That's what we do at the bakery. Either way works fine.

While your dough is proofing, place your baking stone on the lowest rack in your oven, and your cast-iron pan on the highest rack. Preheat the oven to 450°F/ 230°C. Check in on your bread periodically; if the surface feels dried out, spray it with a bit of water to allow for maximum expansion. If it feels cold, make it warmer. This may take up to 2 hours, depending on the conditions of your kitchen. The loaf is ready to go in when it feels very airy and holds a fingerprint when pressed into the surface.

Flip (or gently lift, if you're not using a banneton) the loaves over onto your peel. It might take a couple of batches to bake all your bread, depending on your oven size. Score the face of the loaf with your razor in your desired pattern. Now, grab three ice cubes from the freezer. Being careful to not keep the oven door open too long and let the heat out, open the oven, slide your loaf onto the stone, throw the three ice cubes into the cast-iron pan and close the door. After 5 minutes, quickly open the door and spray the interior of the oven with water. Continue baking until the loaf is evenly browned, about 25 minutes, and has a nice hollow thump when you tap it on the bottom. Let cool for at least 3 hours before cutting.

SEED MIX

YIELD: 1 lb/450 g

4 oz/115 g hulled sunflower seeds

4 oz/115 g hulled sesame seeds

4 oz/115 g yellow millet

2 oz/60 g brown flax

2 oz/60 g rolled rye

Mix all ingredients together in a bowl.

WHOLE WHEAT BAGUETTES
FOR THE HEALTH-CONSCIOUS PARISIAN

If you leave the seed mix out of the Multigrain Bread on page 81, you have a
nice recipe for hearty wheat baguettes. Here's a formula for four loaves that will stay
soft and lovely until dinner in the evening, but they are best enjoyed while still
warm and soft right out of the oven. However you decide to eat them,
they're best the day they're made.

OVERVIEW
- Yield: Four 12 oz/350-g baguettes
- Desired Dough Temperature: 85°F/30°C
- Mixing Time: 40 minutes
- Bulk Fermentation: ~2 hours
- Proofing Time: ~45 minutes
- Baking Time: ~20 minutes
- Cooling Time: ~15 minutes

12 HOURS BEFORE THE BAKE
Mix your biga (see page 29).

6 oz/170 ml 75°F/20°C water

10 oz/280 g white bread flour

¼ tsp/1 g instant yeast

BAKING DAY
6.75 oz/190 g white bread flour

1 oz/30 g whole wheat flour

14.75 oz/420 g biga

1 lb 2.25 oz/520 ml 90°F/32°C water

3 tsp/20 g fine sea salt

¾ tsp/3 g instant yeast

Combine both flours in your large mixing bowl.
In another bowl, mix your biga and water, and
remember to keep that water warm to give your
yeast a comfortable atmosphere to grow. (You should
pull your levain apart with your fingers when adding
it to the water, so it incorporates into the rest of the
ingredients more easily.) Then, dump your flours on
top of the liquid ingredients, and mix it by hand for
about 30 seconds, until it comes together in a shaggy
mass. Don't forget to scrape the bottom and sides of
the bowl regularly; you want all of that flour hydrated
and don't want to see any dry spots. Set aside in a
warm place, at least 80°F/25°C, for 30 minutes. If
you're having trouble finding your warm place, it's
time to use your trusty heat lamp.

Sprinkle the salt and yeast on top of the dough
and grab a four-finger pinch of the dough and pull.
It should stretch out like chunky taffy rather than
just tear off. Incorporate the salt and yeast into the
dough, continuously pushing the sides of the dough
into the middle while turning the bowl. After a minute
of this, the dough should be pulling away from the
sides of the bowl and developing a bit of a sheen, and
you shouldn't feel any crunchy salt crystals. Cover the
bowl, and put it in your warm place for 30 minutes.

Turn your dough onto a lightly floured surface and give it your four-fold (see page 35). It should make a tight little package and after every fold the dough's volume should increase. It should consistently feel warm and active. Roll the dough over and place it, seam side down, back into the bowl. Repeat every 30 minutes (you'll fold the dough three times in total) until the dough is strong but puffy, warm to the touch and holds a fingerprint when pressed into the surface. The whole process will take about 2 hours with a warm kitchen and warm dough.

Once your dough is ready to cut, turn it out onto your floured work surface. Using your bench knife and scale, divide into four 12 ounce/350-g pieces. Gently shape the dough into cylinders (see page 39), being careful not to compress the dough too much, and place seam side down on your work surface. Cover and rest for 20 minutes to build a bit more strength into the loaf before final shaping. Set up a board and couche to receive baguettes (see page 20).

When the 20-minute rest is up, shape the whole wheat dough into four baguettes (see page 40). Be careful not to stretch these shapes out too much, as the nature of whole wheat doughs is that they're structurally weaker than white flour doughs. Think of those bits of bran and germ as sharp little knives that like to chop at any nice gluten structure you've developed with your folding technique. The final baguettes should be 12 inches to 15 inches/30 to 40-cm long, and nice and tapered at the ends. Couche them snugly, seam side up, and place in your warm spot for about 45 minutes.

While your dough is proofing, place your baking stone on the lowest rack in your oven, and your cast-iron pan on the highest rack. Preheat the oven to 450°F/230°C. Check in on your bread periodically; if the surface feels dried out, spray it with a bit of water to allow for maximum expansion. If it feels cold, make it warmer. This may take up to 2 hours, depending on the conditions of your kitchen. The loaf is ready to go in when it feels very airy and holds a fingerprint when pressed into the surface.

Flip the loaves over onto your peel. It might take a couple of batches to bake all your bread, depending on your oven size. You want to make sure not to crowd the baguettes, so two at a time should work just fine. Slash the baguettes with three or four traditional baguette slashes. Now, grab three ice cubes from the freezer. Being careful to not keep the oven door open too long and let the heat out, open the oven, slide your loaf onto the stone, throw the three ice cubes into the cast-iron pan and close the door. After 5 minutes, quickly open the door and spray the interior of the oven with water. Continue baking until the loaf is evenly browned, about 25 minutes, and has a nice hollow thump when you tap it on the bottom. Let cool for at least 3 hours before cutting.

THE AM BREAD BAKER

MORNING BREADS AND FLATBREADS

"What time do you have to get up?" It's one of the most common questions you are asked when people find out you're a baker, and it's generally the first one. Arriving at work with, or way before, the sunrise is as much a hallmark of bakery work as floury jeans, broad shoulders and white lung. But, as you have read, we have night bakers, afternoon bakers, daytime bakers. We have shifts for all types, and all types work those shifts.

But it is undeniable that the bakery must have employees who are ready, willing and able to have the bread shelves properly stocked when retail opens the doors. When we first opened A&J King, I could get away with coming in at 3 a.m. That was before wholesale, and before anyone had ever heard of us. These days, you'll regularly see our morning bread bakers shaping baguettes and traying up cookies at 2:30 a.m. And Saturdays in the summer we come in at 1:30 a.m., and who knows what the future holds.

Before I was forced into being an AM baker, I was a self-diagnosed "night person" and never worked anything but a PM shift. What I quickly discovered was that getting up to an alarm just after midnight is really no more difficult than getting up to an alarm at 6 a.m., 10 a.m. or 2 p.m. Even if it's one of those clocks that plays "whale songs" or "rain on a tin roof," being taken out of a nice dream sucks at any time.

> **❝** The superlatives heaped on the act of baking often stray into hyperbole. Spiritual, empowering, meditative . . . While I appreciate the sentiment, nothing rends a veil like doing it at 3 a.m. for a living. And, while I have, on occasion, genuflected in front of the oven, the gesture has been more profane than pious. Despite this crustiness, the satisfaction gained from baking is undeniable. The yeast is the life; the dough is clay to be shaped. You (and even I) may mutter a prayer when the loaves enter the oven, and shout a hosanna when they emerge. And if you ever wanted to give frankincense and myrrh a run for their money, the smell of cooling loaves is hard to beat. **❞**

JOHN THIBODEAU
AM Baker

But once you're awake, and that first notion that there's a walk-in full of bread to bake hits your brain, you couldn't head back to sleep even if you wanted to. I've known bakers out of the industry for years who still wake up at midnight, paranoid they've overslept. Once the AM baker schedule gets its claws into you, it's there for a long time. Unlike the PM baker, the AM baker has a hard-and-fast deadline. A couple of them, actually. Bread has to be out and cooled for the wholesale driver to bag, and wholesale drivers will, in the most profane of terms usually, let you know if they've been set behind because you hit the snooze button once. And, once the breads are taken care of, retail needs to pack the shelves, and they're not going to be pleased if you lounged in bed for an extra 5 minutes because we *open* in 5 minutes.

If the PM baker experiences the daily pace of the line cook, the AM baker experiences the urgency.

If done properly, however, the shift runs like clockwork and the satisfied, unperturbed baker gets to watch wave after wave of his or her beautifully baked product leave the baking room and enter the arms of grateful customers. If there's time, a brief hobnob with a couple of regulars while getting that first cup of coffee for the day (5 hours into his shift), perhaps a stolen Pain au Chocolat off the pastry display, and then it's on to tomorrow's mix. Gotta get that French in the bowl.

FRENCH BAGUETTES
THE CLASSIC

We call this our "French" dough because we make baguettes and epi out of it, which are synonymous with Parisian bakeries. The baguette is easily our biggest-selling bread item at the bakery. It takes a bit of trying to nail this one down, and it's the bread that will expose the flaws in your style (and equipment) more than any other. Like anything worth doing right, it will try your patience and reward your tenacity. Keep in mind: This dough is mixed significantly cooler than any of the others in the book.

We also make a little extra every time we make this dough, and keep it in a plastic bag in the fridge or freezer. It makes nice pizza dough in a pinch, grilled bread in the summer (just flatten and toss on the grill for a few minutes on each side) and rolls when you need them. It's handy!

OVERVIEW

- Yield: Six 8-oz/250-g baguettes and 1 lb/450 g left over for experimenting
- Desired Dough Temperature: 75˚F/20°C
- Mixing Time: 40 minutes
- Bulk Fermentation: ~2 hours
- Proofing Time: ~45 minutes
- Baking Time: ~25 minutes
- Cooling Time: ~15 minutes

12 HOURS BEFORE THE BAKE

Mix your poolish (see page 27).

7.5 oz/200 ml 75˚F/20°C water

7.5 oz/210 g white bread flour

¼ tsp/1 g instant yeast

BAKING DAY

15 oz/425 g poolish

1 lb 2.5 oz/525 ml 75˚F/20°C water

1 lb 13.75 oz/840 g white bread flour

3 ¼ tsp/23 g fine sea salt

1 tsp/4 g instant yeast

In a large mixing bowl, combine your poolish and water, and remember to keep that water at 75˚F/20°C to give your yeast a comfortable atmosphere to grow, but not grow too fast. Then, dump your flour on top of the liquid ingredients, and mix it by hand for about 30 seconds, until it comes together in a shaggy mass. Don't forget to scrape the bottom and sides of the bowl regularly; you want all of that flour hydrated and don't want to see any dry spots. Set aside in a warm place, at least 80˚F/25°C, for 30 minutes. If you're having trouble finding your warm place, it's time to use your trusty heat lamp.

Sprinkle the salt and yeast on top of the dough and grab a four-finger pinch of the dough and pull. It should stretch out like chunky taffy rather than just tear off. Incorporate the salt and yeast into the dough, continuously pushing the sides of the dough into the middle while turning the bowl. After a minute of this, the dough should be pulling away from the sides of the bowl and developing a bit of a sheen, and you shouldn't feel any crunchy salt crystals. Cover the bowl, and put it in your warm place for 30 minutes.

Turn your dough onto a lightly floured surface and give it your four-fold (see page 35). It should make a tight little package and after every fold the dough's volume should increase. It should consistently feel warm and active. Roll the dough over and place it, seam side down, back into the bowl. Repeat every 30 minutes (you'll fold the dough three times in total) until the dough is strong but puffy, warm to the touch and holds a fingerprint when pressed into the surface. The whole process will take about 2 hours.

Once your dough is ready to cut, turn it out onto your floured work surface. Using your bench knife and scale, divide into six 8-ounce/250-g pieces. Gently preround the dough into cylinders (see page 39), being careful not to compress the dough too much, and place seam side down on your work surface. To make the shaping a bit easier, it's advisable to let the preshaped baguettes cool down before shaping. Place them on a sheet tray and cover with a moist towel. Up to an hour in the refrigerator or on a cold porch should do the trick. While they're resting, set up your couche and your board to receive baguettes (see page 20).

Shape the dough into six 12-inch to 15-inch/30 to 40-cm tapered baguettes (see page 40). Couche them snugly, seam side up, and place in your warm spot for about 45 minutes.

While your dough is proofing, place your baking stone on the lowest rack in your oven, and your cast-iron pan on the highest rack. Preheat the oven to 450°F/230°C. Check in on your bread periodically; if the surface feels dried out, spray it with a bit of water to allow for maximum expansion. If it feels cold, make it warmer. This may take up to 1 hour, depending on the conditions of your kitchen. The loaf is ready to go in when it feels very airy and holds a fingerprint when pressed into the surface.

Flip the loaves over onto your peel. It might take a couple of batches to bake all your bread, depending on your oven size. You want to make sure not to crowd the baguettes, so two or three at a time should work just fine. Slash the baguettes with three or four traditional baguette slashes. Now, grab three ice cubes from the freezer. Being careful to not keep the oven door open too long and let the heat out, open the oven, slide your loaf onto the stone, throw the three ice cubes into the cast-iron pan and close the door. After 5 minutes, quickly open the door and spray the interior of the oven with water. Continue baking until the loaf is evenly browned, about 25 minutes, and has a nice hollow thump when you tap it on the bottom. Let cool for at least 15 minutes before cutting. Warm, crispy baguettes are the best.

FOCACCIA

BREAD AS CANVAS

Like the baguette or ciabatta, focaccia is so universally made that almost every cook has some sort of recipe for it kicking around the kitchen. Its simple list of ingredients—flour, water, olive oil, salt, yeast—makes it attractive to the casual baker, and more power to the folks who use a handed-down recipe. We humbly submit our formula here, and we not-so-humbly think that ours is pretty darn amazing. We think a great focaccia should be crispy, with a wide-open crumb; that the dough should never take a backseat to the toppings; and that if you're not baking it directly on a stone, you're missing out on the soul of this bread. We've suggested several toppings; you can, of course, also devour it plain or concoct your own.

OVERVIEW

- Yield: Six 1-lb/450-g slabs focaccia
- Desired Dough Temperature: 85°F/30°C
- Mixing Time: 40 minutes
- Bulk Fermentation: ~3 hours
- Proofing Time: ~1.5 hours
- Baking Time: ~25 minutes
- Cooling Time: ~15 minutes

12 HOURS BEFORE THE BAKE

Mix your poolish (see page 27).

12.5 oz/350 ml 75°F/20°C water

12.5 oz/350 g white bread flour

½ tsp/2 g instant yeast

BAKING DAY

1 lb 8.75 oz/700 g poolish

1 lb 10.5 oz/740 ml 90°F/32°C water

5 oz/155 ml extra-virgin olive oil

2 lb 4.5 oz/1 kg white bread flour

4 tsp/28 g fine sea salt

1 ¼ tsp/5 g instant yeast

In a large mixing bowl, combine your poolish, water and olive oil, and remember to keep that water warm to give your yeast a comfortable atmosphere to grow. Then, dump your flour on top of the liquid ingredients, and mix it by hand for about 30 seconds, until it comes together in a shaggy mass. Don't forget to scrape the bottom and sides of the bowl regularly; you want all of that flour hydrated and don't want to see any dry spots. Set aside in a warm place, at least 80°F/25°C, for 30 minutes. If you're having trouble finding your warm place, it's time to use your trusty heat lamp.

Sprinkle the salt and yeast on top of the dough and grab a four-finger pinch of the dough and pull. It should stretch out like chunky taffy rather than just tear off. Incorporate the salt and yeast into the dough, continuously pushing the sides of the dough into the middle while turning the bowl. After a minute of this, the dough should be pulling away from the sides of the bowl and developing a bit of a sheen, and you shouldn't feel any crunchy salt crystals. This dough will be significantly looser, or wetter, than other recipes in this book. Cover the bowl, and put it in your warm place for 30 minutes.

Turn your dough onto a lightly floured surface and give it your four-fold (see page 35). It should make a tight little package and after every fold the dough's volume should increase. It should consistently feel warm and active. Roll the dough over and place it, seam side down, back into the bowl. Repeat every 30 minutes (you'll fold the dough four times in total). After the fourth fold, leave the dough alone to develop volume for the last hour; those bubbles are what will make up the nice, open crumb of your focaccia. You're looking for the dough to be strong but puffy, warm to the touch and able to hold a fingerprint when pressed into the surface. The whole process will take about 3 hours.

When the dough is ready to divide, turn it out onto a well-floured work surface—this dough is a bit sticky, so some extra flour is necessary here. Divide it into six 1-pound/450-g pieces, and gently preshape each one into a stubby batard (see page 39). You'll want to keep those edges squared rather than tapered off so you can get a nice rectangular final shape to your focaccia. Let these pieces rest, covered with a cloth, for at least 1 hour.

While your dough is proofing, place your baking stone on the lowest rack in your oven, and your cast-iron pan on the highest rack. Preheat the oven to 450°F/230°C. When the dough is totally relaxed and you can press your finger into the surface and the print holds, you're ready to top and bake them—otherwise known as "the fun part."

It's easiest to top your focaccia slabs right on the peel, so you can easily slide them onto your baking stone. If you're concerned about toppings dropping into the oven, line the peel with parchment paper and shape the focaccia on top of that. While the dough is still on the table, pat a loaf out until it is almost completely flat; then transfer it to the peel. Using your fingertips, dimple the surface while stretching out the dough to form a thin, rough rectangle. Top the focaccia with whatever topping you like (suggestions follow). Now, grab three ice cubes from the freezer. Being careful to not keep the oven door open too long and let the heat out, open the oven, slide your focaccia onto the stone, throw the three ice cubes into the cast-iron pan and close the door. Bake until the exposed crust is golden brown, about 25 minutes. Consume immediately!

TOP YOUR FOCACCIA!

SEA SALT AND HERB

This is a very simple, but classic topping, and there aren't many rules to making it. Before loading your slab into the oven, dimple the surface with your fingers, drizzle with a good olive oil and sprinkle with sea salt, or kosher salt if you don't have sea salt on hand. Only the heartiest of herbs, like rosemary, should go onto the focaccia before you put it into the oven (they can handle the heat and retain aroma after cooking). Otherwise, sprinkle on a few pinches of coarsely chopped fresh herbs of your choice while the loaf is still warm. This topping is not heavy enough to hold the surface down, so you may want to give the dough another 30 minutes or so to proof before throwing it in the oven.

SWEET CORN AND CHERRY

This is such a wonderful topping when it's late summer and corn, cherry tomatoes and basil are in abundance at farm stands or in your garden plot. Toss all of the ingredients together and spread generously on your slab—and leave a few fingersful in the bowl to scoop into your mouth. It's a pre-focaccia amuse bouche.

2 cups/320 g cherry tomatoes, quartered

2 ears corn, kernels cut off the cobs

6 large leaves fresh basil, coarsely chopped

2 tbsp/30 ml extra-virgin olive oil

1 tsp/3 g kosher salt

Mix everything together, spread evenly on the focaccia and bake as directed.

GOLD POTATO AND BLACK PEPPER

Growing potatoes in our garden was a fantastic experiment we tried one recent summer, and it resulted in bags of beautiful spuds that lasted us all of a month. Slice them as thinly as you can for the focaccia, even using a mandolin if you have one. You're looking for the edges to brown and crisp up during their time in the oven. Too-thick slices will just become soggy.

Coarsely ground black pepper

2 to 3 large Yukon Gold potatoes, sliced very thinly (⅛ inch/3 mm)

Extra-virgin olive oil

Dimple the surface of the focaccia, then sprinkle lightly with a layer of black pepper. Layer the potatoes in an overlapping fashion up and down the length of the slab until completely covered. Sprinkle again with black pepper and drizzle lightly with olive oil. Bake until the edges of the potato have curled and browned, and the crust is golden.

ROASTED MUSHROOM AND ONION

There is no doubt that mushrooms, onions and thyme are a combo Andy would put on just about everything if he could. No big surprise that focaccia is pretty awesome with it as well. It got top scores at our focaccia tasting party.

1 ½ lb/700 g mixed fresh mushrooms (button, shitake, oyster and so forth), cut to similar sizes

3 sprigs fresh thyme

1 tbsp/15 g unsalted butter, softened

½ tsp/3 g fine sea salt

1 large onion, peeled and sliced ¼-inch/5-mm thick

Extra-virgin olive oil

Preheat the oven to 400°F/200°C. Toss the mushrooms with the thyme, butter and salt. Arrange in the center of a sheet pan. Place the onions around the mushrooms on the sheet pan and drizzle the onions with olive oil. Roast until the mushrooms and onions start to brown and have lost much of their moisture but are not completely cooked. Cool, and layer the mushrooms and onions on top of your focaccia just before baking.

TOMATO AND DRESSED GREENS

There's a restaurant near our house that offers a "Caesar Salad Pizza" that
we think is just awesome. Hot crustiness with a crisp, cool salad dropped on top—there
you go. It works especially well if you put the greens on the focaccia and serve it
immediately, so you get the full contrast.

**4 or 5 roma tomatoes, or 2 or 3
large heirloom beefsteak tomatoes, sliced ¼-inch/5-mm thick**

Fine sea salt

Extra-virgin olive oil

**Local arugula, mizuna or other
fresh lettuce**

**Red Wine Vinaigrette (page 136)
or your house dressing of choice**

Dimple the surface of the dough with your fingertips and lay the tomatoes down. Do not overlap—they're much too waterlogged to stack on
top of one another. Sprinkle with salt and drizzle with olive oil before
baking; they'll still be moist when the sides of the crust are golden
brown. After removing from the oven, dress your greens with the vinaigrette and pile on top of the still-hot slab. Cut into large slices and serve.

FOUGASSE
THE HOLY HEARTH BREAD

Fougasse is Provence's answer to the Roman-born Focaccia. Their names both come from the Latin root word *focus,* meaning "hearth," and they're both flattened doughs that feature toppings or folded-in ingredients. The distinctive feature of the fougasse is its decorative holes cut into the dough's surface, which are really up to the baker's whim. You've got three flavor variations to choose from here, or you can leave the bread plain. If making olive fougasse, the bread will come out a teeny bit bigger, but that's fine.

OVERVIEW
- Yield: Four 1-lb/450-g fougasse
- Desired Dough Temperature: 85°F/30°C
- Mixing Time: 40 minutes
- Bulk Fermentation: ~3 hours
- Proofing Time: ~1.5 hours
- Baking Time: ~25 minutes
- Cooling Time: ~15 minutes

12 HOURS BEFORE THE BAKE
Mix your biga (see page 29).
9 oz/255 ml 75°F/20°C water
15 oz/425 g white bread flour
¼ tsp/1 g instant yeast

BAKING DAY
1 lb 3.5 oz/550 g biga
1 lb 4.75 oz/590 ml 90°F/32°C water
1 lb 7 oz/650 g white bread flour

3 tsp/22 g fine sea salt
¾ tsp/3 g instant yeast
9.5 oz/290 g kalamata or Sicilian olives, pitted (if making Olive Fougasse)
1 cup/180 g shredded Parmesan or other hard cheese (if making Cheese Fougasse)
½ cup/80 g sunflower seeds and ½ cup/80 g sesame seeds, blended (if making Seeded Fougasse)

In a large mixing bowl, combine your biga and water, and remember to keep that water warm to give your yeast a comfortable atmosphere to grow. (It will help even mixing if you break the biga up into smaller pieces as you add it to the water.) Then, dump your flour on top of the liquid ingredients, and mix it by hand for about 30 seconds, until it comes together in a shaggy mass. Don't forget to scrape the bottom and sides of the bowl regularly; you want all of that flour hydrated and don't want to see any dry spots. Set aside in a warm place, at least 80°F/25°C, for 30 minutes. If you're having trouble finding your warm place, it's time to use your trusty heat lamp.

Sprinkle the salt and yeast on top of the dough and grab a four-finger pinch of the dough and pull. It should stretch out like chunky taffy rather than just tear off. Incorporate the salt and yeast into the dough, continuously pushing the sides of the dough into the middle while turning the bowl. After a minute of this, the dough should be pulling away from the sides of the bowl and developing a bit of a sheen, and you shouldn't feel any crunchy salt crystals (add your olives at this point if you're making Olive Fougasse). This dough will be significantly looser, or wetter, than other dough recipes in this book. Cover the bowl, and put it in your warm place for 30 minutes.

Turn your dough onto a lightly floured surface and give it your four-fold (see page 35). It should make a tight little package and after every fold the dough's volume should increase. It should consistently feel warm and active. Roll the dough over and place it, seam side down, back into the bowl. Repeat every 30 minutes (you'll fold the dough four times in total). After the fourth fold, leave the dough alone to develop volume for the last hour; those bubbles are what will make up the nice, open crumb of your focaccia. You're looking for the dough to be strong but puffy, warm to the touch and able to hold a fingerprint when pressed into the surface. The whole process will take about 3 hours.

When the dough is ready to divide, turn it out onto a well-floured work surface—this dough is a bit sticky, so some extra flour is necessary here. Divide it into four 1-pound/450-g pieces, and gently preshape each one into a round (see page 38). Let these pieces rest, covered with a cloth, for at least 1 hour.

While your dough is proofing, place your baking stone on the lowest rack in your oven, and your cast-iron pan on the highest rack. Preheat the oven to 450°F/230°C. When the dough is totally relaxed and you can press your finger into the surface and the print holds, you're ready to top and bake them.

It's easiest to top your fougasse right on the peel, so you can easily slide them onto your baking stone. If you're concerned about toppings dropping into the oven, line the peel with parchment paper and shape the fougasse on top of that. While the dough is still on the table, pat a loaf out until it is almost completely flat; then transfer it to the peel. Finish patting out until completely flat.

If making Olive Fougasse, no further topping is necessary.

If making Cheese Fougasse, spray your fougasse with water and sprinkle your cheese on top of the loaf, about ¼ cup/45 g per loaf.

If making Seeded Fougasse, spray your fougasse with water and sprinkle an even layer of seeds on top of the loaf, about ¼ cup/40 g per loaf. Top with a pinch of fine sea salt.

Grab your pizza wheel, and cut a pattern of slits into the surface of your dough and spread out evenly with your fingers. There is no shortage of traditional fougasse patterns, but I'm big on dedicating a pattern to a flavor and keeping it consistent.

Now, grab three ice cubes from the freezer. Being careful to not keep the oven door open too long and let the heat out, open the oven, slide your fougasse onto the stone, throw the three ice cubes into the cast-iron pan and close the door. A second spritzing of water into the oven is not necessary unless you're making plain fougasse, as the toppings will keep the surface moist. Bake for about 25 minutes, or until the sides of the crust are golden brown and the toppings have a nice, roasted color (depending on the topping). Eat immediately, or when your mouth can handle the heat.

CIABATTA
CHEWY CRUST, OPEN CRUMB

Everyone knows this classic rustic loaf, but unfortunately, so many factory bakeries make this as an underbaked mess that a lot of folks aren't used to the real deal. We're happy to report, however, that everyone is easily converted after one taste. We like our loaves with dark crusts, and moist and open crumbs, and we also like to make them into a few different shapes. There's the classic pound-and-a-half/700-g ciabatta (which means "slipper" in Italian), ciabattini (little rolls that are perfect for little sandwiches) and long stirato (stretched-out strips of dough used at the bakery for sandwiches). Because this dough is so rustic, it's also very flexible. It can be split up in any way you see fit for your usage; we've given the example of a couple of ciabatta loaves and enough rolls to serve for dinner. If you don't want the rolls, use the extra dough to make stirato.

OVERVIEW

- Yield: Two 1 lb 8 oz/700-g ciabatta, plus eight 4-oz/100-g ciabattini or four 8-oz/250-g stirato
- Desired Dough Temperature: 85°F/30°C
- Mixing Time: 40 minutes
- Bulk Fermentation: ~3 hours
- Proofing Time: ~1 hour
- Baking Time: ~25 minutes
- Cooling Time: ~15 minutes

12 HOURS BEFORE THE BAKE

Mix your biga (see page 29).

9.25 oz/260 ml 75°F/20°C water

15.5 oz/440 g white bread flour

½ tsp/2 g instant yeast

BAKING DAY

1 lb 11 oz/765 g white bread flour

2.25 oz/60 g whole wheat flour

1 lb 8.75 oz/700 g biga

1 lb 9.25 oz/715 ml 90°F/32°C water

3 ½ tsp/25 g fine sea salt

1 tsp/4 g instant yeast

Combine your flours in your large mixing bowl. In another bowl, mix your biga and water, and remember to keep that water warm to give your yeast a comfortable atmosphere to grow. (You should pull your biga apart with your fingers when adding it to the water so it incorporates into the rest of the ingredients more easily.) Then, dump your flours on top of the liquid ingredients, and mix it by hand for about 30 seconds, until it comes together in a shaggy

mass. Don't forget to scrape the bottom and sides of the bowl regularly; you want all of that flour hydrated and don't want to see any dry spots. Set aside in a warm place, at least 80°F/25°C, for 30 minutes. If you're having trouble finding your warm place, it's time to use your trusty heat lamp.

Sprinkle the salt and yeast on top of the dough and grab a four-finger pinch of the dough and pull. It should stretch out like chunky taffy rather than just tear off. Incorporate the salt and yeast into the dough, continuously pushing the sides of the dough into the middle while turning the bowl. After a minute of this, the dough should be pulling away from the

sides of the bowl and developing a bit of a sheen, and you shouldn't feel any crunchy salt crystals. Cover the bowl, and put it in your warm place for 30 minutes.

Turn your dough onto a lightly floured surface and give it your four-fold (see page 35). It should make a tight little package and after every fold the dough's volume should increase. It should consistently feel warm and active. Roll the dough over and place it, seam side down, back into the bowl. Repeat every 30 minutes (you'll fold the dough four times in total). After the fourth fold, leave the dough alone to develop volume for the last hour; those bubbles are what will make up the nice, open crumb of your ciabatta. You're looking for the dough to be strong but puffy, warm to the touch and able to hold a fingerprint when pressed into the surface. The whole process will take about 3 hours with a warm kitchen and warm dough.

Shaping ciabatta is easy because there's no shaping involved, only cutting. Once your dough has risen, turn it out onto your floured work surface. Using your bench knife and scale, cut two large rectangles out of the dough. You're looking for them to weigh 1 pound 8 ounces/700 g, but you'll only know how good your guesswork is when you put the loaf on the scale. If you need to rip off or add on pieces, that's fine; just add your pieces to the middle of the rectangle. As a guide, they should be about 5 inches × 10 inches/12 × 25 cm.

If you're making ciabattini, cut the remaining strips of dough into 4-ounce/100-g squares, again placing the smaller "correction" pieces right in the middle. Place the ciabatta and the ciabattini loaves on a well-floured couche and pleat them snugly. To make stirato, just cut off 3-inch × 12-inch/7 × 30-cm strips of dough and lay them onto a floured couche, as you would baguettes. Pleat them snugly. All of these options will take about 1 hour to proof in your warm kitchen.

While your dough is proofing, place your baking stone on the lowest rack in your oven, and your cast-iron pan on the highest rack. Preheat the oven to 450°F/230°C. Check in on your bread periodically; if the surface feels dried out, spray it with a bit of water to allow for maximum expansion. If it feels cold, make it warmer. This may take up to an hour, depending on the conditions of your kitchen. The loaf is ready to go in when it feels very airy and holds a fingerprint when pressed into the surface.

Gently flip the loaves over and place onto your peel (See? The extra pieces are now hidden underneath the loaf. Nice and tidy.) It might take a couple of batches to bake all your bread, depending on your oven size. Ciabatta are easy in this sense as well—no slashing is necessary to create the classic "old slipper" look.

Now, grab three ice cubes from the freezer. Being careful to not keep the oven door open too long and let the heat out, open the oven, slide your loaf onto the stone, throw the three ice cubes into the cast-iron pan and close the door. After 5 minutes, quickly open the door and spray the interior of the oven with water. Continue baking until the loaf is evenly browned, about 25 minutes, and has a nice hollow thump when you tap it on the bottom. If you're baking ciabattini or stirato, the total baking time will be more like 15 minutes, to keep your crust soft for sandwiches. Let cool for at least 30 minutes before cutting.

CORNMEAL-PUMPKIN HEARTH BREAD
THE FARM STAND SPECIAL

As soon as school starts in the fall, we begin fielding calls from customers asking when this bread will be back on the shelves. It has a limited life cycle in the bakery, as we bake it during the couple of months when we can source the pumpkins from nearby farms. Notice that we call for corn flour, which has a finer grind than cornmeal and absorbs liquid better, resulting in a smoother final crumb. You can find it in specialty grocery stores and online.

This bread has a sweet, moist and tighter crumb than some of the other breads we make, and the crust has a bit more give. It makes amazing toast and grilled cheese sandwiches, its yellow hue crisping to a beautiful golden in the pan. You can easily shape these into loaf pans for more convenient sandwich slices; we make them as pumpkinesque rounds.

OVERVIEW
- Yield: Three 1 lb 10 oz/750-g loaves
- Desired Dough Temperature: 85°F/30°C
- Mixing Time: 40 minutes
- Bulk Fermentation: ~2 hours
- Proofing Time: ~2 hours
- Baking Time: ~25 minutes
- Cooling Time: ~1 hour

12 HOURS BEFORE THE BAKE
Mix your poolish (see page 27).
15 oz/425 ml 75°F/20°C water
15 oz/425 g bread flour
½ tsp/2 g instant yeast

BAKING DAY
1 lb 4.75 oz/590 g white bread flour
8.75 oz/250 g corn flour

1 lb 13.5 oz/840 g poolish
8.75 oz/250 ml 90°F/32°C water
8.75 oz/250 g roasted pumpkin (see page 106)
2.25 oz/70 ml extra-virgin olive oil
1.5 oz/40 g honey
3 ½ tsp/25 g fine sea salt
1 ¼ tsp/5 g instant yeast

Combine your flours in your large mixing bowl. In another bowl, mix your poolish, water, roasted pumpkin, olive oil and honey, and remember to keep that water warm to give your yeast a comfortable atmosphere to grow. Swirl those ingredients around with your hand to combine. Then, dump your flours on top of the liquid ingredients, and mix it by hand for about 30 seconds, until it comes together in a shaggy mass. Don't forget to scrape the bottom and sides of the bowl regularly; you want all of that flour hydrated and don't want to see any dry spots. Set aside in a warm place, at least 80°F/25°C, for 30 minutes. If you're having trouble finding your warm place, it's time to use your trusty heat lamp.

Sprinkle the salt and yeast on top of the dough and grab a four-finger pinch of the dough and pull. It should stretch out like chunky taffy rather than just tear off. Incorporate the salt and yeast into the dough, continuously pushing the sides of the dough into the middle while turning the bowl. After a minute of this, the dough should be pulling away from the sides of the bowl and developing a bit of a sheen, and you shouldn't feel any crunchy salt crystals. Cover the bowl, and put it in your warm place for 30 minutes.

Turn your dough onto a lightly floured surface and give it your four-fold (see page 35). It should make a tight little package and after every fold the dough's volume should increase. It should consistently feel warm and active. Roll the dough over and place it, seam side down, back into the bowl. Repeat every 30 minutes (you'll fold the dough three times in total) until the dough is strong but puffy, warm to the touch and holds a fingerprint when pressed into the surface. The whole process will take about 2 hours.

Once your dough is ready to cut, turn it out onto your floured work surface. Using your bench knife and scale, divide into three 1 pound 10 ounce/750-g pieces. Gently shape the dough into rounds (see page 38), being careful not to compress the dough too much, and place seam side down on your work surface. Cover and rest for 20 minutes to build a bit more strength into the loaf before final shaping. Dust three bannetons with corn flour.

Take your rested rounds and gently but firmly shape them into rounds again. If your seams feel like they're coming undone when you lift the loaf up, give it a few minutes sitting seam side down on the table to seal it, and next time, use less flour for shaping. The dough's moisture should be enough to seal the loaf closed. Place your shaped loaves seam side up in your bannetons, cover with a cloth or plastic wrap and place in your trusty warm spot.

While your dough is proofing, place your baking stone on the lowest rack in your oven, and your cast-iron pan on the highest rack. Preheat the oven

to 450°F/230°C. Check in on your bread periodically; if the surface feels dried out, spray it with a bit of water to allow for maximum expansion. If it feels cold, make it warmer. This may take up to 2 hours, depending on the conditions of your kitchen. The loaf is ready to go in when it feels very airy and holds a fingerprint when pressed into the surface.

Flip the loaves over onto your peel. It might take a couple of batches to bake all your bread, depending on your oven size. Slash the surface of the loaves in your desired pattern. Now, grab three ice cubes from the freezer. Being careful to not keep the oven door open too long and let the heat out, open the oven, slide your loaf onto the stone, throw the three ice cubes into the cast-iron pan and close the door. After 5 minutes, quickly open the door and spray the interior of the oven with water. Continue baking until the loaf is evenly browned, about 25 minutes, and has a nice hollow thump when you tap it on the bottom. Let cool for at least 1 hour before cutting.

ROASTED PUMPKIN

The best pumpkins for this recipe are the smaller ones called sugar pumpkins. Choose those that are 8 inches to 10 inches/20 to 25 cm in diameter. Wash any remaining field dirt off the surface, and knock the stem off with a hammer. Bisect the pumpkin top to bottom (starting at the stem) and scoop out the seeds. Place the two halves cut side down on a sheet pan and roast at 400°F/200°C until the skin starts to collapse and a skewer passes through the flesh easily, 45 to 60 minutes. Let cool, and then scoop the roasted flesh off the skins. Refrigerate until ready to use. Remember to warm the pumpkin to room temperature before using in this recipe (or else you'll sandbag your dough temperature), and squish it through your fingers to smooth it out a bit before incorporating it into the other ingredients.

ROASTED POTATO, ONION AND ROSEMARY BREAD
THE SAVORY FENDU

We love this product because it fills the bakeshop with the aroma of stuffing. We're not sure if it's just the onions and rosemary, or whether the potatoes add more than just texture and moisture to the dough, but wow, it smells like Thanksgiving every time. We shape the loaves as fendu, which means "split" in French, and you'll need a thin rolling pin or a 1-inch/2.5-cm diameter dowel (from any local hardware store) to give them their distinctive, bi-hemispherical look. This is a fantastic cold-weather bread, perfect for dipping in stews or mopping up juices from any cut of roast meat.

OVERVIEW

- Yield: Three 1 lb 10 oz/750-g loaves
- Desired Dough Temperature: 85°F/30°C
- Mixing Time: 40 minutes
- Bulk Fermentation: ~2 hours
- Proofing Time: ~1.5 hours
- Baking Time: ~25 minutes
- Cooling Time: ~1 hour

12 HOURS BEFORE THE BAKE

Mix your poolish (see page 27).

12 oz/340 ml 75°F/20°C water

12 oz/340 g bread flour

½ tsp/2 g instant yeast

BAKING DAY

1 lb 5.75 oz/620 g white bread flour

6 oz/170 g whole wheat flour

8 oz/250 g roasted Yukon Gold potatoes, crushed (see page 109)

1 lb 7 oz/650 g poolish

14 oz/400 ml 90°F/32°C water

5.5 oz/155 g roasted onions (see page 109)

3 ¼ tsp/23 g tsp fine sea salt

1 ¼ tsp/5 g instant yeast

1 small bunch fresh rosemary, chopped

Combine your flours and potatoes in your large mixing bowl. In another bowl, mix your poolish, water and onions, and remember to keep that water warm to give your yeast a comfortable atmosphere to grow. Swirl those ingredients around with your hand to combine. Then, dump your flour and potatoes on top of the liquid ingredients, and mix it by hand for about 30 seconds, until it comes together in a shaggy mass. If there are still larger chunks of potatoes in the mix, just crush them between your fingers. Don't forget to scrape the bottom and sides of the bowl regularly; you want all of that flour hydrated and don't want to see any dry spots. Set aside in a warm place, at least 80°F/25°C, for 30 minutes. If you're having trouble finding your warm place, it's time to use your trusty heat lamp.

Sprinkle the salt and yeast on top of the dough and grab a four-finger pinch of the dough and pull. It should stretch out like chunky taffy rather than just tear off. Incorporate the salt and yeast into the dough, continuously pushing the sides of the dough into the middle while turning the bowl. After a minute of this, the dough should be pulling away from the sides of the bowl and developing a bit of a sheen, and you shouldn't feel any crunchy salt crystals. Add the rosemary to the mix, and continue mixing by hand until well incorporated. Remember, the folding will help distribute the rosemary, so don't wear yourself out getting it perfectly mixed in. Cover the bowl, and put it in your warm place for 30 minutes.

Turn your dough onto a lightly floured surface and give it your four-fold (see page 35). It should make a tight little package and after every fold the dough's volume should increase. It should consistently feel warm and active. Roll the dough over and place it, seam side down, back into the bowl. Repeat every 30 minutes (you'll fold the dough three times in total) until the dough is strong but puffy, warm to the touch and holds a fingerprint when pressed into the surface. The whole process will take about 2 hours.

Once your dough is ready to cut, turn it out onto your floured work surface. Using your bench knife and scale, divide into three 1 pound 10 ounce/750-g pieces. Gently shape the dough into rounds (see page 38), being careful not to compress the dough too much, and place seam side down on your work surface. Cover and rest for 1 hour. Dust three bannetons with flour and set aside.

For this particular style, the fendu (see page 39), we call the next step "pinning" rather than "shaping," because, well, that's what it is. Dust your work surface with a good amount of flour, and gently scoop your rounded loaves up with your bench knife and place— still seam side down!—on the flour. Sprinkle some flour on the top of the loaf as well. Grab the thinnest rolling pin you have, such as a French one or a 1-inch/2.5-cm diameter dowel, and press down in the middle of the loaf. Roll the pin back and forth a bit, not pressing so hard that you actually cut through the dough, and then remove the pin to reveal a bisected loaf. Roll the two sides together, gently flip the loaf over and place cut side down in the banneton. Place the finished loaves in your warm place and cover with a towel.

While your dough is proofing (what bakers call the last rise of a shaped loaf), place your baking stone on the lowest rack in your oven, and your cast-iron pan on the highest rack. Preheat the oven to 450°F/230°C. Check in on your bread periodically; if the surface feels dried out, spray it with a bit of water to allow for maximum expansion. If it feels cold, make it warmer. This may take up to 1 ½ hours, depending on the conditions of your kitchen. The loaf is ready to go in when it feels very airy and holds a fingerprint when pressed into the surface.

Flip the loaves out of the bannetons and onto your peel. It might take a couple of batches to bake all your bread, depending on your oven size. Now, grab three ice cubes from the freezer. Being careful to not keep the oven door open too long and let the heat out, open the oven, slide your loaf onto the stone, throw the three ice cubes into the cast-iron pan and close the door. After 5 minutes, quickly open the door and spray the interior of the oven with water. Continue baking until the loaf is evenly browned, about 25 minutes, and has a nice hollow thump when you tap it on the bottom. Let cool for at least an hour before cutting.

ROASTED POTATOES AND ROASTED ONIONS

It's always a great idea to roast a few more potatoes and onions than you will need. You'll eat about a quarter of the potatoes, and you can throw caramelized onions in everything from your omelet tomorrow to your roasted chicken's pan sauce.

1 lb/450 g Yukon Gold potatoes, cut into 1-in/2.5-cm dice

1 lb/450 g yellow onions, trimmed and sliced into ½-in/1-cm strips

Extra-virgin olive oil

Salt and freshly ground black pepper

Preheat the oven to 400°F/200°C. Toss the potatoes and the onions on separate sheet pans with a drizzle of olive oil and a bit of salt and pepper. Roast, stirring regularly, for about 45 minutes or until the onions are browned and the potatoes are crispy, golden and soft in the middle. Let cool fully, and crush the potatoes roughly with your hands, before using in the bread. If making ahead and refrigerating, bring them to room temperature before adding them to your dough.

SEMOLINA-APRICOT BREAD
SWEET, GOLDEN AND EASY LIKE SUNDAY MORNING

Semolina flour comes from durum wheat, a strain of the same stuff that produces your bread flour. Unfortunately, it has a pretty paltry amount of gluten in it, o it's generally mixed with white flour when used in bread (it's amazingly fantastic for pasta, though). When used in dough, it imparts a beautiful yellow glow and a firm toothiness to the crumb that pairs nicely with dried fruit—in this case, apricots. The fennel just makes it smell delicious, making this one of our most popular Sunday morning breads.

OVERVIEW
- Yield: Four 1 lb 4 oz/550-g loaves
- Desired Dough Temperature: 85°F/30°C
- Mixing Time: 40 minutes
- Bulk Fermentation: ~2 hours
- Proofing Time: ~1 hour
- Baking Time: ~25 minutes
- Cooling Time: ~1 hour

12 HOURS BEFORE THE BAKE
Mix your poolish (see page 27).
11.5 oz/330 ml 75°F/20°C water
11.5 oz/330 g white bread flour
½ tsp/2 g instant yeast

BAKING DAY
15.5 oz/440 g white bread flour
14.5 oz/410 g semolina flour
1 lb 6.5 oz/640 g poolish
1 lb/450 ml 90°F/32°C water
3 ½ tsp/24 g fine sea salt
1 ½ tsp/6 g instant yeast
10.25 oz/290 g dried apricots, diced
1 ½ tbsp/18 g fennel seeds

Combine your flours in your large mixing bowl. In another bowl, mix your poolish and water, and remember to keep that water warm to give your yeast a comfortable atmosphere to grow. Then, dump your flour on top of the liquid ingredients, and mix it by hand for about 30 seconds, until it comes together in a shaggy mass. Don't forget to scrape the bottom and sides of the bowl regularly; you want all of that flour hydrated and don't want to see any dry spots. Set aside in a warm place, at least 80°F/25°C, for 30 minutes. If you're having trouble finding your warm place, it's time to use your trusty heat lamp.

Sprinkle the salt and yeast on top of the dough and grab a four-finger pinch of the dough and pull. It should stretch out like chunky taffy rather than just tear off. Incorporate the salt and yeast into the dough, continuously pushing the sides of the dough into the middle while turning the bowl. After a minute of this, the dough should be pulling away from the sides of the bowl and developing a bit of a sheen, and you shouldn't feel any crunchy salt crystals. Toss in your apricots and fennel seeds, and, using the same arm motion, incorporate them into the dough. Remember, the folds will help distribute everything, so don't wear yourself out getting the apricots perfectly mixed. Cover the bowl, and put it in your warm place for 30 minutes.

Turn your dough onto a lightly floured surface and give it your four-fold (see page 35). It should make a tight little package and after every fold the dough's volume should increase. It should consistently feel warm and active. Roll the dough over and place it, seam side down, back into the bowl. Repeat every 30 minutes (you'll fold the dough three times in total) until the dough is strong but puffy, warm to the touch and holds a fingerprint when pressed into the surface. The whole process will take about 2 hours.

Once your dough is ready to cut, turn it out onto your floured work surface. Using your bench knife and scale, divide into four 1 pound 4 ounce/550-g pieces. Gently shape the dough into rounds (see page 38), being careful not to compress the dough too much, and place seam side down on your work surface. Cover and rest for 20 minutes to build a bit more strength into the loaf before final shaping. Dust the couche lightly with semolina flour.

Take your rested rounds and gently, but firmly, shape them into 12-inch/30-cm tapered batards (see page 39). Pinch the seam shut if necessary, but the dough's moisture should be enough to seal the loaf closed. Place your shaped loaves seam side up on your couche, and pleat snugly. Place the board in your warm spot until the loaves are ready to bake.

While your dough is proofing, place your baking stone on the lowest rack in your oven, and your cast-iron pan on the highest rack. Preheat the oven to 450°F/230°C. Check in on your bread periodically; if the surface feels dried out, spray it with a bit of water to allow for maximum expansion. If it feels cold, make it warmer. This may take over an hour, depending on the conditions of your kitchen. The loaf is ready to go in when it feels very airy and holds a fingerprint when pressed into the surface.

Flip the loaves over onto your peel. It might take a couple of batches to bake all your bread, depending on your oven size. Slash the surface of the loaves in your desired pattern—we do a classic one-slash right along the length of the entire loaf. Now, grab three ice cubes from the freezer. Being careful to not keep the oven door open too long and let the heat out, open the oven, slide your loaf onto the stone, throw the three ice cubes into the cast-iron pan and close the door. After 5 minutes, quickly open the door and spray the interior of the oven with water. Continue baking until the loaf is evenly browned, about 25 minutes, and has a nice hollow thump when you tap it on the bottom. Let cool for at least 1 hour before cutting.

CINNAMON SWIRL BREAD
MAKE A TOAST!

This is a classic pan loaf that just gets better when toasted and spread with butter or used for French toast. There are a few keys to making this loaf perfectly: You need to scald the milk to denature the proteins that inhibit the bread rising; you need to use ice instead of water to cool the milk down; and you need to fold the dough only once, rather than the usual three or four times, so as not to build too much strength into the dough. You will be rolling it up tightly, after all, and you don't want the layers to separate. The final key? Lots and lots of cinnamon sugar.

OVERVIEW

- Yield: Two 5-in × 9-in/12 × 23-cm pan loaves
- Desired Dough Temperature: 85°F/30°C
- Mixing Time: 40 minutes
- Bulk Fermentation: ~2 hours
- Proofing Time: ~2 hours
- Baking Time: ~25 minutes
- Cooling Time: ~15 minutes

BAKING DAY

1 lb 12.75 oz/815 g white bread flour

3.75 oz/110 g granulated sugar

6.5 oz/180 ml whole milk

6.5 oz/180 g ice

6 oz/170 g large eggs

3.25 oz/90 g unsalted butter, melted

2 ½ tsp/17 g fine sea salt

2 tsp/8 g instant yeast

⅓ cup/40 g ground cinnamon and ⅓ cup/60 g granulated sugar, mixed together

Combine your flour and sugar in your large mixing bowl. Warm your milk in a pan on the stove or in the microwave until it is steaming, and then pour it into a large bowl and combine with the ice to make a (relatively) room-temperature liquid. Add the eggs and melted butter, and swish the mixture around with your hand to mix it up, making sure to break all of the yolks. Then, dump your flour and sugar on top of the liquid ingredients, and mix it by hand for about 30 seconds, until it comes together in a shaggy mass. Don't forget to scrape the bottom and sides of the bowl regularly; you want all of that flour hydrated and don't want to see any dry spots. Set aside in a warm place, at least 80°F/25°C, for 30 minutes. If you're having trouble finding your warm place, it's time to use your trusty heat lamp.

Sprinkle the salt and yeast on top of the dough and grab a four-finger pinch of the dough and pull. It should stretch out like chunky taffy rather than just tear off. Incorporate the salt and yeast into the dough, continuously pushing the sides of the dough into the middle while turning the bowl. After a minute of this, the dough should be pulling away from the sides of the bowl and developing a bit of a sheen, and you shouldn't feel any crunchy salt crystals. Cover the bowl, and put it in your warm place for 1 hour.

Turn your dough onto a lightly floured surface and give it your four-fold (see page 35). The fold will happen just once. You're actually looking to just build a little strength into the dough here, not a whole lot. You are going to be rolling in a layer of cinnamon sugar for the final shape, and you don't want to create so much strength that the layers separate when popped in the oven. So, after the fold, wait another hour, and if your kitchen's at a nice, warm temperature, you're now ready to divide.

Turn the dough out onto your floured work surface; it should be a little sloppy. Using your bench knife and scale, divide into two 1 pound 12 ounce/800-g pieces. Gently preshape the dough into loose 8-inch to 10-inch/20 to 25-cm cylinders (see page 39), and cover with cloth or plastic so they can relax for the final shaping. This will take about 1 hour. When the pieces are relaxed enough where you can pat them out and they won't go springing back, they're ready to shape.

Orient the piece of dough so that the skinnier ends are at the top and bottom of your work surface, and pat out with your hands until they're about ¼-inch/5 mm thick. Spray the surface of the dough down with water, and, leaving a ½ inch/1 cm rim around the perimeter (you'll need those clean edges to seal the perimeter shut when you're done shaping), sprinkle a layer of cinnamon sugar on the dough so that you can't see the dough underneath, but no more. This should be about ⅓ cup/50 g per loaf.

Starting at the end of the dough closest to you, roll the dough up—but don't just fold it over itself. Stretch some tension into the surface of the dough, and when you get to the end, pinch the seam shut so that you have a nice, tight cylinder with a smooth surface. Place the shaped loaves into oiled 5-inch × 9-inch/12-cm × 23-cm loaf pans, and cover with a cloth.

While your dough is proofing, place your baking stone on the lowest rack in your oven, and your cast-iron pan on the highest rack. Preheat the oven to 400°F/200°C. Check in on your bread periodically; if the surface feels dried out, spray it with a bit of water to allow for maximum expansion. If it feels cold, make it warmer. This may take up to 2 hours, depending on the conditions of your kitchen. The loaf is ready to go in when the dome of the loaf has risen about 2 inches/5 cm above the lip of the pan.

Spray the surface of the loaves one last time with a few spritzes of water. Now, grab three ice cubes from the freezer. Being careful to not keep the oven door open too long and let the heat out, open the oven, slide your loaves onto the stone, throw the three ice cubes into the cast-iron pan and close the door. After 5 minutes, quickly open the door and spray the interior of the oven with water. Continue baking until the loaf is an even golden brown, about 25 minutes. Remove the loaves from the pans immediately and place on a cooling rack for at least 30 minutes before cutting. If the sides and bottom seem too light after removing the pans, feel free to place them back in the oven for 5 minutes to firm up the crust.

ANADAMA BREAD
BORN AND BREAD LOCALLY

Unlike all of the European breads that are made at the bakery, Anadama is a local favorite—and we mean real local. As far as anyone knows, this particular bread—made with wheat, corn and molasses—originated just a 30-minute drive north of the bakery, in the small fishing community of Rockport, Massachusetts. There's no more official Anadama bakery anymore (it closed in 1972), but the recipe is carried on by any true New England bakery worth its salt. Not being from the area, we didn't initially offer it, but quickly caved to pressure. We're glad we did, and are thrilled to be part of such a local tradition.

OVERVIEW

- Yield: Two 1 lb 12 oz/800 g 5-in × 9-in/12 × 23-cm pan loaves
- Desired Dough Temperature: 85˚F/30°C
- Mixing Time: 40 minutes
- Bulk Fermentation: ~2 hours
- Proofing Time: ~2 hours
- Baking Time: ~25 minutes
- Cooling Time: ~3 hours

BAKING DAY

1 lb 8 oz/680 g white bread flour

6.5 oz/180 g corn flour

1 lb 3.25 oz/550 ml 90˚F/32°C water

1.25 oz/35 g unsalted butter, softened

4.75 oz/130 g blackstrap molasses

2 tsp/14 g fine sea salt

1 ¼ tsp/5 g instant yeast

Combine the flours in your large mixing bowl. In another bowl, mix your water, butter and molasses, swishing everything around with your fingers to disperse. Make sure to keep your water warm to give your yeast a nice, warm atmosphere to grow. Dump your flours on top of the liquid ingredients, and mix it by hand for about 30 seconds, until it comes together in a shaggy mass. Don't forget to scrape the bottom and sides of the bowl regularly; you want all of that flour hydrated and don't want to see any dry spots. Set aside in a warm place, at least 80˚F/25°C, for 30 minutes. If you're having trouble finding your warm place, it's time to use your trusty heat lamp.

Sprinkle the salt and yeast on top of the dough and grab a four-finger pinch of the dough and pull. It should stretch out like chunky taffy rather than just tear off. Incorporate the salt and yeast into the dough, continuously pushing the sides of the dough into the middle while turning the bowl. After a minute of this, the dough should be pulling away from the sides of the bowl and developing a bit of a sheen, and you shouldn't feel any crunchy salt crystals. Cover the bowl, and put it in your warm place for 30 minutes.

Turn your dough onto a lightly floured surface and give it your four-fold (see page 35). It should make a tight little package and after every fold the dough's volume should increase. It should consistently feel warm and active. Roll the dough over and place it, seam side down, back into the bowl. Repeat every 30 minutes (you'll fold the dough three times in total) until the dough is strong but puffy, warm to the touch and holds a fingerprint when pressed into the surface. The whole process will take about 2 hours with a warm kitchen and warm dough.

Once your dough is ready to cut, turn it out onto your floured work surface. Using your bench knife and scale, divide into two 1 pound 12 ounce/800-g pieces. Gently shape the dough into rounds (see page 38), being careful not to compress the dough too much, and place seam side down on your work surface. Cover and rest for 20 minutes to build a bit more strength into the loaf before final shaping.

Next, lightly oil two 5-inch × 9-inch/12 × 23-cm bread pans and set them to the side. Take your rested rounds and gently, but firmly, shape them into stubby cylinders (see page 39), leaving them seam side down on the table. Place your shaped loaves seam side down in your loaf pans, cover with a damp cloth or plastic wrap and place in your trusty warm spot.

While your dough is proofing, place your baking stone on the lowest rack in your oven, and your cast-iron pan on the highest rack. Preheat the oven to 400˚F/200°C. Check in on your bread periodically; if the surface feels dried out, spray it with a bit of water to allow for maximum expansion. If it feels cold, make it warmer. This may take up to 2 hours, depending on the conditions of your kitchen. The loaf is ready to go in when it feels very airy and holds a fingerprint when pressed into the surface.

When you're ready to bake, score the face of the loaf with four or five diagonal slashes. This releases tension in two directions, so when the oven spring occurs, you get a nice, even expansion of the surface of the loaf. Now, grab three ice cubes from the freezer. Being careful to not keep the oven door open too long and let the heat out, open the oven, slide your loaves onto the stone, throw the three ice cubes into the cast-iron pan and close the door. After 5 minutes, quickly open the door and spray the interior of the oven with water. Continue baking until the loaf is evenly browned, about 30 minutes, and has a nice hollow when you tap it on the bottom. Immediately, but carefully, remove the loaves from the pans and place them on a cooling rack. If the sides and bottom of the loaf look light, feel free to pop them back in the oven for a few minutes. Let cool for at least 3 hours before cutting.

SUNFLOWER-RYE BREAD

SEED BREAD FOR THE BIRDS

This hearty bread requires that you make not only a starter 12 hours in advance, but a soaker as well. This softens up the rye flakes (which should be available at your nearest natural foods store) and keeps them from absorbing too much of the water in the mix. Note: This is a stickier dough than many others in the book. If it still seems wet after adding the salt and yeast, that's fine. The strength will come when you fold, and excess liquid will be absorbed.

OVERVIEW

- Yield: Three 1 lb 12 oz/800-g loaves
- Desired Dough Temperature: 85°F/30°C
- Mixing Time: 40 minutes
- Bulk Fermentation: ~2 hours
- Proofing Time: ~1 hour
- Baking Time: ~25 minutes
- Cooling Time: ~1 hour

12 HOURS BEFORE THE BAKE

Mix your poolish
10 oz/280 ml 75°F/20°C water
10 oz/280 g white bread flour
½ tsp/2 g instant yeast
Mix your soaker
8.75 oz/250 ml 75°F/20°C water
7 oz/200 g rye flakes

BAKING DAY

1 lb 10.5 oz/750 g white bread flour

7 oz/200 g hulled sunflower seeds, plus ¾ cup/120 g for garnish

18.5 oz/520 g poolish

10.5 oz/300 ml 90°F/32°C water

Soaker (all)

0.5 oz/15 g honey

3 ¼ tsp/23 g tsp fine sea salt

1 tsp/4 g instant yeast

Combine your flour and the 7 oz/200 g sunflower seeds in your large mixing bowl. In another bowl, combine your poolish, water, soaker and honey, and remember to keep that water warm to give your yeast a comfortable atmosphere to grow. Then, dump your flours on top of the liquid ingredients, and mix it by hand for about 30 seconds, until it comes together in a shaggy mass. Don't forget to scrape the bottom and sides of the bowl regularly; you want all of that flour hydrated and don't want to see any dry spots. Set aside in a warm place, at least 80°F/25°C, for 30 minutes. If you're having trouble finding your warm place, it's time to use your trusty heat lamp.

Sprinkle the salt and yeast on top of the dough and grab a four-finger pinch of the dough and pull. It should stretch out like chunky taffy rather than just tear off. Incorporate the salt into the dough, continuously pushing the sides of the dough into the middle while turning the bowl. After a minute of this, the dough should be pulling away from the sides of the bowl and developing a bit of a sheen, and you shouldn't feel any crunchy salt crystals. Cover the bowl, and put it in your warm place for 30 minutes.

Turn your dough onto a lightly floured surface and give it your four-fold (see page 35). It should make a tight little package and after every fold the dough's volume should increase. It should consistently feel warm and active. Roll the dough over and place it, seam side down, back into the bowl. Repeat every 30 minutes for the first 2 hours (you'll fold the dough three times in total) until the dough is strong but puffy, warm to the touch and holds a fingerprint when pressed into the surface. The whole process will take about 2 hours with a warm kitchen and warm dough.

Once your dough is ready to cut, turn it out onto your floured work surface. Using your bench knife and scale, divide into three 1 pound 10 ounce/750-g pieces. Gently shape the dough into rounds (see page 38), being careful not to compress the dough too much, and place seam side down on your work surface. Cover and rest for 20 minutes to build a bit more strength into the loaf before final shaping. Set up your couche and proofing board.

Next, take your rested rounds and shape each loaf into tapered batards (see page 39). If your seams feel like they're coming undone when you lift the loaf up, feel free to pinch the seams shut with your fingers. Spray the surface of each loaf, and roll them in the ¾ cup/120 g sunflower seeds. Place each loaf on the unfloured couche, seeds down, and pleat cozily.

While your dough is proofing (what bakers call the last rise of a shaped loaf), place your baking stone on the lowest rack in your oven, and your cast-iron pan on the highest rack. Preheat the oven to 425°F/220°C. Check in on your bread periodically; if the surface feels dried out, spray it with a bit of water to allow for maximum expansion. If it feels cold, make it warmer. This may take up to 3 hours, depending on the conditions of your kitchen. The loaf is ready to go in when it feels very airy and holds a fingerprint when pressed into the surface.

Flip the loaves over onto your peel. It might take a couple of batches to bake all your bread, depending on your oven size. Score the face of the loaf with your razor in your desired pattern. Now, grab three ice cubes from the freezer. Being careful to not keep the oven door open too long and let the heat out, open the oven, slide your loaf onto the stone, throw the three ice cubes into the cast-iron pan and close the door. After 5 minutes, quickly open the door and spray the interior of the oven with water. Continue baking until the loaf is evenly browned, about 25 minutes, and has a nice hollow thump when you tap it on the bottom. Let cool for at least 30 minutes before cutting.

OATMEAL-CINNAMON-RAISIN LOAVES
THE SATURDAY MORNING SPECIAL

This is the perfect weekend loaf. Sweet and moist, it's great for eating with butter, toasting with jam and making into French toast. We sell more of these loaves on Saturday morning than almost any other bread in the bakery. They come out of the oven just after we open, so early risers can grab them warm right off the shelves. And regulars have been known to prepay and hang around waiting for the announcement that they're ready to sell. Or, you can be like Mrs. Harrington, who has called us and asked to have two loaves set aside for her every Saturday for the past 5 years. We should rename it the Harrington Bread!

OVERVIEW

- Yield: Four 1 lb 4 oz/550-g loaves
- Desired Dough Temperature: 85°F/30°C
- Mixing Time: 40 minutes
- Bulk Fermentation: ~2 hours
- Proofing Time: ~2 hours
- Baking Time: ~25 minutes
- Cooling Time: ~1 hour

BAKING DAY

2 lb .75 oz/1 kg white bread flour

3 tbsp/14 g ground cinnamon

1 lb 9.25 oz/715 ml 110°F/40°C water

5.5 oz/155 g rolled oats, plus 1 cup/80 g for garnish

2 oz/60 g honey

2 ¾ tsp/19 g fine sea salt

2 ¾ tsp/11 g instant yeast

11.5 oz/330 g raisins, soaked in hot water for 20 minutes and well drained

Combine your flour and cinnamon in your large mixing bowl. In another bowl, combine your hot water and 5.5 ounces/155 g rolled oats, allowing the oats to absorb the liquid for 10 minutes or until the water temperature drops to about 90°F/32°C. Add the honey, and swish the ingredients around with your hand to combine. Then, dump your flour and cinnamon on top of the liquid ingredients, and mix it by hand for about 30 seconds, until it comes together in a shaggy mass. Don't forget to scrape the bottom and sides of the bowl regularly; you want all of that flour hydrated and don't want to see any dry spots. Set aside in a warm place, at least 80°F/25°C, for 30 minutes. If you're having trouble finding your warm place, it's time to use your trusty heat lamp.

Sprinkle the salt and yeast on top of the dough and grab a four-finger pinch of the dough and pull. It should stretch out like chunky taffy rather than just tear off. Incorporate the salt and yeast into the dough, continuously pushing the sides of the dough into the middle while turning the bowl. After a minute of this, the dough should be pulling away from the sides of the bowl and developing a bit of a sheen, and you shouldn't feel any crunchy salt crystals. Add your raisins and continue that incorporating action until everything is evenly distributed. Remember, the folds will help distribute the raisins, so don't wear yourself out mixing them all in perfectly. Cover the bowl, and put it in your warm place for 30 minutes.

Turn your dough onto a lightly floured surface and give it your four-fold (see page 35). It should make a tight little package and after every fold the dough's volume should increase. It should consistently feel warm and active. Roll the dough over and place it, seam side down, back into the bowl. Repeat every 30 minutes (you'll fold the dough three times in total) until the dough is strong but puffy, warm to the touch and holds a fingerprint when pressed into the surface. The whole process will take about 2 hours. This dough is a bit denser than some others, so if you want to leave it in your warm spot for another half hour to rise a bit more, we wouldn't blame you.

Once your dough is ready to cut, turn it out onto your floured work surface. Using your bench knife and scale, divide into four 1 pound 4 ounce/550-g pieces. Gently shape the dough into rounds (see page 38), being careful not to compress the dough too much, and place seam side down on your work surface. Cover and rest for 20 minutes to build a bit more strength into the loaf before final shaping. Set up your proofing board and couche.

Then, take your rested rounds and gently, but firmly, shape them into stubby batards (see page 39)—with this dough, it's a little like shaping stretchy clay. If your seams feel like they're coming undone when you lift the loaf up, give it a few minutes sitting seam side down on the table to seal it, and next time, use less flour for shaping. The dough's moisture should be enough to seal the loaf closed. Spray the surface of each loaf with water and roll the top of each loaf in the 1 cup/80 g rolled oats, then place seam side up (oats side down) on an unfloured couche. Pleat the loaves snugly, and place in a warm area.

While your dough is proofing, place your baking stone on the lowest rack in your oven, and your cast-iron pan on the highest rack. Preheat the oven to 450°F/230°C. Check in on your bread periodically; if the surface feels dried out, spray it with a bit of water to allow for maximum expansion. If it feels cold, make it warmer. This may take up to 2 hours, depending on the conditions of your kitchen. The loaf is ready to go in when it feels very airy and holds a fingerprint when pressed into the surface.

Flip the loaves over onto your peel. It might take a couple of batches to bake all your bread, depending on your oven size. Slash the surface of the loaves in your desired pattern; we use an alternating diagonal pattern that really increases the volume in all directions. Now, grab three ice cubes from the freezer. Being careful to not keep the oven door open too long and let the heat out, open the oven, slide your loaf onto the stone, throw the three ice cubes into the cast-iron pan and close the door. After 5 minutes, quickly open the door and spray the interior of the oven with water. Continue baking until the loaf is evenly browned, about 25 minutes, and has a nice hollow thump when you tap it on the bottom. Let cool for at least 1 hour before cutting.

PAIN DE MIE

WHITE BRED WHITE BREAD

Pain de mie means "bread of the crumb," because it's baked so that the crust is a light golden brown rather than the classic deep russet of other artisan loaves. It's basically the way the French get to enjoy what most folks in America regard as "normal" bread. There's a very soft spot in our hearts for white bread. It's what we grew up on, and it absolutely has its place in the pantheon of breads. Fried baloney just doesn't work on a crusty baguette or sourdough.

OVERVIEW

- Yield: Two 1 lb 8 oz/700 g 5-in × 9-in/12 ×23-cm pan loaves
- Desired Dough Temperature: 85°F/30°C
- Mixing Time: 40 minutes
- Bulk Fermentation: ~2 hours
- Proofing Time: ~1 hour
- Baking Time: ~25 minutes
- Cooling Time: 1 hour

BAKING DAY

1 lb 10 oz/740 g white bread flour

0.75 oz/20 g granulated sugar

2 ½ tsp/17 g fine sea salt

1 lb 1.75 oz/500 ml 90°F/32°C water

1.25 oz/35 g milk powder

1.25 oz/35 g unsalted butter, melted

2 ½ tsp/10 g instant yeast

This mixing procedure is a little different from the rest of the breads, so please pay attention! Combine your flour, sugar and salt in your large mixing bowl. Mix with your hands to combine. In another bowl, mix your water, milk powder, butter and yeast. Swish them together to dissolve the milk powder and yeast, and remember to keep that water warm to give your yeast a comfortable atmosphere to grow. Then, dump your dry ingredients on top of the liquid ingredients, and mix it by hand for about 30 seconds, until it comes together in a shaggy mass. Don't forget to scrape the bottom and sides of the bowl regularly; you want all of that flour hydrated and don't want to see any dry spots. Note: There's no autolyse for this dough. It's moving right off the bat.

Turn your dough onto a lightly floured surface and give it your four-fold (see page 35). It should make a tight little package and after every fold the dough's volume should increase. It should consistently feel warm and active. Roll the dough over and place it, seam side down, back into the bowl. Repeat every 30 minutes (you'll fold the dough three times in total) until the dough is strong but puffy, warm to the touch and holds a fingerprint when pressed into the surface. The whole process will take about 2 hours.

Turn the dough out onto your floured work surface; it should be very pillowy. Using your bench knife and scale, divide into two 1 pound 8 ounce/700-g pieces. Gently shape the dough into loose rounds (see page 38). Cover and rest for 20 minutes to build a bit more strength into the loaf before final shaping.

Next, lightly oil two 5-inch × 9-inch/12 × 23-cm bread pans and set them to the side. Take your rested rounds and gently, but firmly, shape them into stubby cylinders (see page 39) and place your shaped loaves seam side down in your loaf pans. Cover with a damp cloth or plastic wrap, and place in your trusty warm spot.

While your dough is proofing, place your baking stone on the lowest rack in your oven, and your cast-iron pan on the highest rack. Preheat the oven to 400°F/200°C. Check in on your bread periodically; if the surface feels dried out, spray it with a bit of water to allow for maximum expansion. If it feels cold, make it warmer. This may take up to 2 hours, depending on the conditions of your kitchen. You might not want to stick your finger into the surface of this particular loaf—it gets pretty light and airy, and you don't want to deflate it.

Spray the surface of the loaves one last time with a few spritzes of water, score them with four or five diagonal slashes along the surface and slide them onto your peel.

Now, grab three ice cubes from the freezer. Being careful to not keep the oven door open too long and let the heat out, open the oven, slide your loaf onto the stone, throw the three ice cubes into the cast-iron pan and close the door. After 5 minutes, quickly open the door and spray the interior of the oven with water. Continue baking until the loaf is an even golden brown, about 25 minutes. Remove the loaf from the pan immediately and place on a cooling rack for at least 30 minutes before cutting. If the sides and bottom seem too light after removing the pan, feel free to place it back in the oven for 5 minutes.

BACON AND BLACK PEPPER BREAD
PORK AND SPICE MAKES EVERYTHING NICE

Full disclosure by Andy: I had bacon in many, many more recipes in this book, but I was voted down by Jackie. I'm just saying. Anyway, smoky, thick-cut bacon and black pepper is one of my favorite flavor combinations in the whole wide world, so it makes sense that they would somehow make their way into a loaf of bread. I couldn't bear to toss all of that flavorful bacon fat from the roasting pan, so in that went as well—and before you say "gross," a traditional bread spread served at a local Polish restaurant is rendered lard speckled with bacon bits, and it's amazing. Trust me.

OVERVIEW

- Yield: Three 1 lb 8 oz/700-g loaves
- Desired Dough Temperature: 85°F/30°C
- Mixing Time: 40 minutes
- Bulk Fermentation: ~2 hours
- Proofing Time: ~1 hour
- Baking Time: ~25 minutes
- Cooling Time: ~1 hour

12 HOURS BEFORE THE BAKE

Mix your poolish (see page 27).

10.5 oz/300 ml 75°F/20°C water

10.5 oz/300 g white bread flour

½ tsp/2 g instant yeast

Roast bacon (see page 125)

BAKING DAY

1 lb 8 oz/680 g white bread flour

2 oz/60 g corn flour

1 lb 4.75 oz/600 g poolish

1 lb 1 oz/480 ml 90°F/32°C water

2 oz/50 g bacon fat, rendered

2 tsp/15 g fine sea salt

1 tsp/4 g instant yeast

5 oz/140 g roasted bacon, diced (see page 125)

2 tbsp/30 g coarsely ground black pepper

Combine your flours in your large mixing bowl. In another bowl, mix your poolish, water and bacon fat, and remember to keep that water warm to give your yeast a comfortable atmosphere to grow. Then, dump your flour on top of the liquid ingredients, and mix it by hand for about 30 seconds, until it comes together in a shaggy mass. Don't forget to scrape the bottom and sides of the bowl regularly; you want all of that flour hydrated and don't want to see any dry spots. Set aside in a warm place, at least 80°F/25°C, for 30 minutes. If you're having trouble finding your warm place, it's time to use your trusty heat lamp.

Sprinkle the salt and yeast on top of the dough and grab a four-finger pinch of the dough and pull. It should stretch out like chunky taffy rather than just tear off. Incorporate the salt and yeast into the dough, continuously pushing the sides of the dough into the middle while turning the bowl. After a minute of this, the dough should be pulling away from the sides of the bowl and developing a bit of a sheen, and you shouldn't feel any crunchy salt crystals. Toss in your bacon and pepper, and, using the same arm motion, incorporate them into the dough. Remember, the folds will help distribute everything, so don't wear yourself out getting that bacon perfectly mixed. Cover the bowl, and put it in your warm place for 30 minutes.

Turn your dough onto a lightly floured surface and give it your four-fold (see page 35). It should make a tight little package and after every fold the dough's volume should increase. It should consistently feel warm and active. Roll the dough over and place it, seam side down, back into the bowl. Repeat every 30 minutes (you'll fold the dough three times in total), until the dough is strong but puffy, warm to the touch and holds a fingerprint when pressed into the surface. The whole process will take about 2 hours.

Once your dough is ready to cut, turn it out onto your floured work surface. Using your bench knife and scale, divide into three 1 pound 8 ounce/700-g pieces. Gently shape the dough into rounds (see page 38), being careful not to compress the dough too much, and place seam side down on your work surface. Cover and rest for 20 minutes to build a bit more strength into the loaf before the final shaping. Find your couche and proofing board, and dust the couche lightly with flour.

Take your rested rounds and gently but firmly shape them into 15-inch/40-cm tapered batards (see page 39). Pinch the seam shut if necessary, but the dough's moisture should be enough to seal the loaf closed. Place your shaped loaves seam side up on your couche, and pleat snugly. Place the board in your warm spot until they're ready to bake.

While your dough is proofing, place your baking stone on the lowest rack in your oven, and your cast-iron pan on the highest rack. Preheat the oven to 450°F/230°C. Check in on your bread periodically; if the surface feels dried out, spray it with a bit of water to allow for maximum expansion. If it feels cold, make it warmer. This may take over an hour, depending on the conditions of your kitchen. The loaf is ready to go in when it feels very airy and holds a fingerprint when pressed into the surface.

Flip the loaves over onto your peel. It might take a couple of batches to bake all your bread, depending on your oven size. Slash the surface of the loaves in your desired pattern. Now, grab three ice cubes from the freezer. Being careful to not keep the oven door open too long and let the heat out, open the oven, slide your loaf onto the stone, throw the three ice cubes into the cast-iron pan and close the door. After 5 minutes, quickly open the door and spray the interior of the oven with water. Continue baking until the loaf is evenly browned, about 25 minutes, and has a nice hollow thump when you tap it on the bottom. Let cool for at least 1 hour before cutting.

ROASTED BACON

We've found that the easiest way to cook bacon is to roast it—and it ensures that you don't mistakenly burn bits of bacon in the fat and ruin the taste. You'll need about 10 pieces of the thickest-cut bacon you can find. Arrange it in a single layer on a sheet pan, and roast at 400°F/200°C for about 15 minutes, or until golden and crispy. Drain on paper towels and cool before dicing, and don't forget to save the fat for the mix!

THE BAKER'S LUNCH

SANDWICHES AND DELICIOUS FROM-SCRATCH FILLINGS

We put things on bread because it's the perfect canvas to feature well-prepared ingredients. It's the unsung hero of the sandwich world, which is ironic because it's what makes those slices of cheese and meat a sandwich to begin with. Yet so many delis out there pay so much attention to the stuffing and skimp on the bread. And there's no fancy deli-sliced meat or expensive cheese that won't be sandbagged by the spongy, dry crust of a mass-produced sandwich roll. I'd rather just have fillings on a plate than suffer through crappy bread.

At the bakery, we serve an assortment of predesigned sandwiches that are pretty much based on what we like to eat. Almost every selection is one we ate at the bakery long before we offered sandwiches for sale. We'd bring in leftovers from dinner, throw them on a baguette and eat while working. The term *baker's lunch* arose from the wide variety of items (usually brought from home) that a busy baker can chuck in between two pieces of well-crafted artisan bread and have it serve as a meal. Some of our favorites are so simple they don't even warrant recipes here: A pickle and Sriracha sauce. A smooshed banana and Nutella. A fried egg and cilantro.

Any of the sandwiches we offer here can be made with any type of bread. We've noted which breads we serve them on at the bakery, though our customers like to switch things up. We tend to put softer or more delicate fillings, like smoked salmon, on stirato, and sturdier fillings on baguette. And we put turkey on Multigrain. Turkey just works best with that grainy crunch.

In addition to the bread, we look for bold flavors that complement each other—something rich, something acidic, something fresh. And, whenever possible, make your ingredients from scratch. It makes your creation all the more delicious, not to mention unique. We've included recipes for easily made ingredients and, as an added bonus, recipes for five of our favorite in-house pickles. These recipes are our favorites and serve as guides (delicious, delicious guides), but after you've warmed up a bit, feel free to experiment with the ingredients. Make a sandwich that's your very own.

THE FRENCH HAM

It's so simple that it's almost not worth having a recipe for it. But it's this type of sandwich that most often satisfies the baker midshift. Nothing beats the simplicity of good cheese and good meat on good bread; the French know that all too well. That's why we call this the French Ham. It's worth repeating one of the bakery's mantras: If you're going to go simple, you have to go high-quality. Go to a real cheese counter, and get your ham at a high-end market.

YIELD: 1 sandwich

½ **of a baguette (about 7 inches/ 18 cm; see page 58, 84 or 89)**

3 or 4 thick slices Brie cheese, room temperature

3 oz/75 g thinly sliced smoked ham

Slice the baguette lengthwise, layer the cheese and ham in the middle, close your eyes and pretend you're in the Latin Quarter of Paris.

OUR BANH MI

When I lived in San Francisco, almost every day for lunch I would grab this fantastic sandwich on crispy bread from the local Asian grocer, made with all sorts of rich meats, pickled vegetables and fresh cilantro. That was my first experience with the banh mi, and when we decided to serve sandwiches at the bakery, it was an obvious choice. We make our pickled vegetables and mayonnaise in-house and use smoked ham instead of the traditional pâté or head cheese (no one would let me boil a pig's head at the bakery). We don't serve it with hot sauce, but a few squirts of sriracha put this sandwich over the top.

YIELD: 1 sandwich

HOMEMADE MAYONNAISE

Yield: About 2 ½ cups/550 g

2 cups/470 ml canola oil

2.4 oz/70 g pasteurized egg yolks (or fresh, if you're sure of their quality)

¾ tsp/5 g fine sea salt

¾ tsp/2 g dry mustard

1 ½ tbsp/20 ml white wine vinegar

PICKLED VEGETABLES

Yield: Enough for about 8 sandwiches

1 medium daikon radish, peeled and thinly sliced

2 large carrots, peeled and thinly sliced

1 hot chile pepper of your choice, thinly sliced (optional)

2 cups/500 ml hot water

3 cups/710 ml white wine vinegar

⅓ cup/60 g granulated sugar

½ of a baguette (about 7 inches/18 cm; see page 58, 84 or 89)

3 oz/85 g smoked ham, thinly sliced

3 or 4 pieces thinly sliced cucumber

Fresh cilantro leaves

To make the mayonnaise, in a large metal bowl, whisk together everything but the canola oil until well combined. Add the oil in a very slow, steady stream, while still whisking, until the emulsification begins (it helps to hold the bowl still with a couple of damp kitchen towels on the counter, rolled to form a little doughnut-shaped stand). Once the mixture begins to thicken, you can add the oil a little faster, but be careful—when mayonnaise "breaks" (or separates), it can't be fixed. You have to start over, which is a huge bummer. Refrigerate for up to 1 week.

To make the pickles, dissolve the sugar in the hot water and add the vinegar. Cover the sliced vegetables with the brine. Store in the refrigerator for at least 24 hours before using.

To assemble the banh mi, slice the baguette lengthwise and spread on the mayonnaise. Layer on the ham, pickled vegetables, cucumber and cilantro.

SMOKED SALMON STIRATO

With its smoky aroma and soft texture, smoked salmon can tend to dominate. We find that the composition of this sandwich works quite well in terms of tempering its taste and texture without hiding it. The spicy, crisp daikon sprouts add a refreshing touch, as does the cool, acidic crème fraiche. The onions are another strong component that can stand up to the salmon and help keep it humble. Don't worry, though: The salmon finds an ally in the briny capers. Use leftover crème fraîche anywhere you might use sour cream.

YIELD: 1 sandwich

CRÈME FRAÎCHE
Yield: 2 ¼ cups/530 ml

2 cups/480 ml heavy cream

¼ cup/60 ml cultured buttermilk

½ of a stirato (about 7 inches/ 18 cm; page 101)

Capers

3 oz/85 g smoked salmon

Daikon sprouts

Red onion, thinly sliced

To make the crème fraîche, combine the cream and buttermilk, and leave in a warm place for 24 hours to culture. It should smell pleasingly sour and nutty when finished and have thickened noticeably. Refrigerate until set; it will keep for about 1 week.

To assemble the sandwich, slice the stirato lengthwise and spread on the crème fraîche. Stick the capers to this layer to prevent them from rolling all over your counter. Layer on the salmon, daikon sprouts and red onion.

THE UN-MASSACHUSETTS ROAST BEEF SANDWICH

The North Shore of Massachusetts feels like the roast beef capital of the world. You can't drive for 10 minutes up here without passing a Kelly's, Sammy's, Nick's, Bill and Bob's or another first-name drive-through roast beef joint. We pass four on the way home every day. So we tried our hand at a unique roast beef sandwich, and although you can't get it "with au jus," as they say, it is Jackie's favorite of all the sandwiches we serve at the bakery. The key to getting that pink through-and-through look to your beef is to cook it "slow and low," and we've included an easy recipe to do just that.

YIELD: 1 sandwich

PICKLED RED ONIONS
Yield: About 1 pint/260 g

2 large red onions, peeled, halved and sliced into ¼-inch/5-mm strips

3 cups/710 ml white wine vinegar

1 tbsp/12 g granulated sugar

SUPER-SLOW ROAST BEEF
Yield: Enough for 10 to 12 sandwiches

1 top round roast, about 5 lbs/2 kg

Salt and freshly ground black pepper

OVEN-DRIED TOMATOES
Yield: Enough for 10 to 12 sandwiches

10 roma tomatoes

Kosher salt

Extra-virgin olive oil

½ of a baguette (about 7 inches/ 18 cm; see page 58, 84 or 89)

2 pieces sliced sharp cheddar cheese

To make the pickled onions, dissolve the sugar in the vinegar, and pour over the onions. Refrigerate for 24 hours or until the onions take on a neon-pink hue; that's how you know they're ready. They'll keep for 2 weeks in the refrigerator.

To make the roast beef, heat the oven to 200°F/90°C. Generously salt the exterior of the roast beef, and add pepper to your taste. Place on a rack on a sheet pan, and cook until the internal temperature reaches 125°F/50°C. This may take 4 hours depending on the size of the roast. Let cool completely before slicing.

To make the tomatoes, trim the stem ends off the tomatoes, and slice ¼ inch/5-mm thick. Lay the pieces flat on a parchment-lined sheet pan, and sprinkle with kosher salt. Roast for 1 hour in the 200°F/90°C oven, or until significantly dried but not crispy. To store, arrange the tomatoes flat in an airtight container, cover with olive oil and refrigerate. They'll keep for about 1 week.

To assemble the sandwich, layer the roast beef, cheddar slices, tomatoes and pickled red onion onto the sliced baguette.

SALAD SANDWICH

We like salad, but it never satisfied us as a lunch item. A salad thrown between a couple of slices of fancy bread, however, fills me up every time. The fresher and more in season your vegetables are, the better. If you can grab the tomatoes, cucumbers and greens out of your backyard garden, well then, that's the best way to enjoy it. Toss the greens in a respectable amount of vinaigrette (use more for hearty greens, less for delicate ones), and let the feta add the rest of the salt.

YIELD: 1 sandwich

RED WINE VINAIGRETTE
Yield: About 2 cups/470 ml

1 cup/240 ml extra-virgin olive oil

⅔ cup/160 ml red wine vinegar

1 tsp/0.5 g dried oregano

1 tsp/2 g Dijon mustard

½ tsp/3 g fine sea salt

½ of a stirato (about 7 inches/ 18 cm; see page 101)

A couple of handfuls of mixed greens of your choice

Tomato, cored and sliced

Cucumber, peeled and sliced

Crumbled feta cheese

To make the vinaigrette, combine everything and whisk. Boom—easy vinaigrette. Feel free to substitute vinegars, fresh herbs or anything else you have convenient in your refrigerator. Make it yours!

To assemble the sandwich, slice the stirato lengthwise, and split the bread open almost as if you're making an open-face sandwich. Sprinkle both halves lightly with vinaigrette, then layer the tomato slices, cucumber and feta cheese onto the bread. In a separate bowl, toss the greens with another light sprinkle of dressing, then pile them onto the bread. Pressing a long knife or spatula into the middle of the bread to secure the greens, fold the sandwich shut. This method makes it easier to fill and handle.

CRAN-TURKEY ON MULTIGRAIN

With only three ingredients, this is one of the simplest sandwiches we have, but each component is so strongly flavored that we found we didn't need to dress it up much. The cranberry sauce will keep for a couple of weeks in your refrigerator and can also be used as a spread on toast or biscuits, an extra addition to corn bread or spooned warm over grilled pork tenderloin. If you can get your cranberries fresh in the fall (Massachusetts is full of cranberry bogs), all the better, but frozen ones work as well. Just cook the sauce a little longer.

YIELD: 1 sandwich

CRANBERRY SAUCE

1 lb/450 g fresh or frozen cranberries

10.5 oz/300 g granulated sugar

Juice and zest of 1 navel orange

2 slices Multigrain Bread (page 81)

4 oz/100 g smoked turkey breast, sliced

Fresh chèvre

To make the cranberry sauce, combine all ingredients except the zest in a heavy-bottom saucepan. Mix everything to combine. Cook over medium heat, stirring occasionally to prevent scorching, until the berries start to pop, about 20 minutes. Remove from the heat and stir in the zest. Cool, cover and refrigerate to let firm up.

To assemble the sandwich, layer the turkey on one half of the multigrain, and spoon cranberry sauce on top. Spread a thick layer of goat cheese on the other half and close it up. Simple!

MARINATO

This sandwich came about from a container of leftovers. We had made a particularly chunky pasta sauce the night before and taken the leftovers to work. After downing the pasta, there was a good deal of chunky sauce still left in the container . . . so onto some bread it went. Add some cheese and house-roasted red peppers, and we have our Marinato. By the way, the sauce is still good over pasta, so feel free to use the leftovers that way.

YIELD: 1 sandwich

MARINATO SAUCE

Yield: Enough for 6 sandwiches

2 lb/1 kg grape tomatoes (about 3 pints/1 kg)

3 garlic cloves, minced

½ small red onion, diced

4 oz/100 g black or green pitted olives (or a mix), coarsely chopped

2 tbsp/30 ml extra-virgin olive oil

2 tbsp/30 ml balsamic vinegar

½ tsp/1.5 g kosher salt

ROASTED RED PEPPERS

Yield: Enough for 6 sandwiches

3 large red bell peppers

2 garlic cloves, peeled

Extra-virgin olive oil

½ of a stirato (about 7 inches/ 18 cm; see page 101)

Fresh mozzarella cheese, sliced

3 or 4 fresh basil leaves

To make the Marinato Sauce, heat the oven to 350°F/180°C. Combine all ingredients in a shallow saucepan. Roast for 30 to 40 minutes, stirring occasionally, until the tomatoes pop and the surface begins to dry. Do not overcook—a chunky sauce is the goal here.

You can roast your red peppers two ways: For a firmer pepper, place directly on the flame of a gas stove, and, rotating regularly, singe each side until the surface of the entire pepper is black. Alternatively, for a softer pepper, place on a sheet pan and roast in a 425°F/220°C oven until the pepper is collapsed and blackened, about 30 to 40 minutes. Either way, place the hot peppers in a bowl and completely cover with plastic wrap. As the peppers cool, the skins will steam off. Hold the cooled peppers under running water to remove the skins, and pull out the seeds and stem. Slice the peppers into ½-inch/1-cm strips and store in a container, covered in olive oil. Crush the garlic cloves and store in the oil with the peppers.

To assemble the sandwich, split the stirato lengthwise and spoon about ⅔ cup/160 ml of the Marinato Sauce onto the bread. Layer the mozzarella and red peppers on top, and garnish with the basil leaves.

THE WARIEL

There's no special house-made prep that goes into this sandwich, but it obtained such a following among the bakers that we now have to keep a jar of hot crushed red peppers (that pickled spread that you can get on your Italian sub at pizza joints) on hand just in case anyone gets a hankering. The sandwich is named after longtime pastry baker Mariel, whom we called, when she was in a rare bad mood, Wariel. This sandwich has a ton of spicy and sour elements, but it's a zinger when you need a pick-me-up.

YIELD: 1 sandwich

½ of a baguette (about 7 inches/ 18 cm; see page 58, 84 or 89)

Dijon mustard

Mayonnaise

Crushed red pepper paste

3 oz/75 g smoked ham, thinly sliced

2 slices sharp cheddar cheese

Diced sour pickles

Sliced red onions

Split the baguette down the middle, and spread on the mustard, mayonnaise and crushed red pepper paste. Layer on the ham and cheese, then add the pickles and onions.

PICKLES

Andy has loved pickles since he was a kid, and was over-the-moon excited when he realized we could custom-make them for the bakery. It's one of his favorite things that we prepare from scratch, and even though they're not difficult, they represent one of those little things that make our humble sandwich station unique. Many local farm stands carry pickling cucumbers throughout the summer, and it's best to use those rather than regular slicing cukes. They're firmer and have fewer seeds, thus allowing them to stand up much better to an acidic brine. Or, better yet, pick a variety of vegetables to brine. Again, firmer ones work better, so it's a great way to preserve carrots, green beans, cauliflower or other surprise bumper-crop items from your garden.

Keep in mind that these aren't lacto-fermented pickles; they're what we call a quick pickle. This is when brines based on vinegar, water, salt, sugar and herbs or spices are poured over your vegetable of choice and left to soak under refrigeration. They'll be ready in as little as 24 hours, but will become stronger and more flavorful a few days after that. These are the types of pickles Andy is obsessed with. Go big or go home, as the old saying goes.

Each recipe of brine is made to cover about 2 pounds/1 kg of produce, depending on how they're sliced. Thinly sliced "chips" will pack a jar more tightly than spears or chunks, for example. A couple of experiments will inform you as to your favorite option.

Always use hot water, and dissolve your salt and sugar before adding the vinegar. Add your spices to the heated brine, and pour over the vegetables. Cool and store, covered, in your refrigerator. Eat after 24 hours; enjoy for a few weeks after that. Or, for longer storage, pack into sterilized mason jars, follow standard canning procedure and keep them on your shelf.

Happy pickling!

DILL-MUSTARD PICKLES

YIELD: 3 or 4 pint/470-ml jars, depending on cut used

2 lbs/1 kg pickling cucumbers or firm vegetables of your choice

1 small bunch fresh dill

4 ½ cups/1 ml hot water

⅓ cup/16 g kosher salt

⅔ cup/130 g granulated sugar

5 ½ cups/1.3 ml white wine vinegar

¼ cup/40 g mustard seeds

2 tbsp/14 g ground mustard

Cut your vegetables and layer them with the dill in a 1-gallon/4-L container, or divide among three or four pint/470-ml jars if you're planning on keeping them in your canning pantry. Dissolve the sugar and salt in the hot water, then add the vinegar and spices to the brine. If you're going with bulk storage, pour the brine over the vegetables, cool and store, covered, in your refrigerator for at least 24 hours before eating. If you're using the pint jars, pour the brine into each individual container and process in a boiling hot water bath for 10 minutes before cooling.

SPICY GARLIC SOUR PICKLES

YIELD: 3 or 4 pint/470-ml jars, depending on cut used

2 lbs/1 kg pickling cucumbers or firm vegetables of your choice

15 garlic cloves, coarsely chopped

4 large jalapeno chiles, sliced, seeded if desired

3 cups/710 ml hot water

⅓ cup/16 g kosher salt

⅓ cup/60 g granulated sugar

6 cups/1.5 L white wine vinegar

Cut your vegetables and layer them with the garlic and jalapenos in a 1-gallon/4-L container, or divide among three or four pint/470-ml jars if you're planning on keeping them in your canning pantry. Dissolve the sugar and salt in the hot water, then add the vinegar to the brine. If you're going with bulk storage, pour the brine over the vegetables, cool and store, covered, in your refrigerator for at least 24 hours before eating. If you're using the pint jars, pour the brine into each individual container and process in a boiling hot water bath for 10 minutes before cooling.

BREAD AND BUTTER SPEARS

YIELD: 3 pint/470-ml jars

2 lbs/1 kg pickling cucumbers or firm vegetables of your choice

1 small red onion, sliced

8 cups/2 ml cider vinegar

1 cup/240 ml hot water

1 tbsp/8 g celery seeds

1 tsp/2 g whole cloves

3 cups/570 g granulated sugar

½ cup/24 g kosher salt

Cut your vegetables and layer them with the red onions in a 1-gallon/4-L container, or divide among three or four pint/470-ml jars if you're planning on keeping them in your canning pantry. Heat the vinegar, water and spices on the stove, and dissolve the sugar and salt into the mixture to make your brine. If you're going with bulk storage, pour the brine over the vegetables, cool and store, covered, in your refrigerator for at least 24 hours before eating. If you're using the pint jars, pour the brine into each individual container and process in a boiling hot water bath for 10 minutes before cooling.

SMOKY, SWEET, SPICY PICKLES

YIELD: 3 or 4 pint/470-ml jars, depending on cut used

2 lbs/1 kg pickling cucumbers or firm vegetables of your choice

2 cups/470 ml hot water

1 ¼ cups/250 g brown sugar

½ cup/24 g kosher salt

3 ½ cups/830 ml cider vinegar

3 ½ cups/830 ml white wine vinegar

5 chipotle chiles in adobo sauce, sliced

2 tbsp/30 ml adobo sauce

2 tsp/5 g ground cumin

2 tsp/5 g paprika

Cut your vegetables and layer them in a 1-gallon/4-L container, or divide among three or four pint/470-ml jars if you're planning on keeping them in your canning pantry. Dissolve the sugar and salt in the hot water, then add the vinegar, chipotle peppers, adobo sauce and spices to the brine. If you're going with bulk storage, pour the brine over the vegetables, cool and store, covered, in your refrigerator for at least 24 hours before eating. If you're using the pint jars, pour the brine into each individual container and process in a boiling hot water bath for 10 minutes before cooling.

SWEET LEMON-BASIL PICKLES

YIELD: 3 or 4 pint/470-ml jars, depending on cut used

2 lbs/1 kg pickling cucumbers or firm vegetables of your choice

Zest of 3 lemons

1 small bunch fresh basil

6 cups/1.5 L hot water

1 ½ cups/290 g granulated sugar

⅓ cup/16 g kosher salt

3 cups/710 ml white wine vinegar

Juice of 3 lemons

Cut your vegetables and layer them with the lemon zest and basil in a 1-gallon/4-L container, or divide among three or four pint/470-ml jars if you're planning on keeping them in your canning pantry. Dissolve the sugar and salt in the hot water, then add the vinegar and lemon juice to the brine. If you're going with bulk storage, pour the brine over the vegetables, cool and store, covered, in your refrigerator for at least 24 hours before eating. If you're using the pint jars, pour the brine into each individual container and process in a boiling hot water bath for 10 minutes before cooling.

THE AM PASTRY BAKER

CROISSANTS, STICKY BUNS AND BREAD PUDDING

Bakers' schedules, as we've mentioned, are very much laid out before their shift even starts. Bread-centric employees know they'll be bouncing from corner to corner of the room, with longish pauses at the shaping bench or in front of the oven, and then back again to the bench, and so on. It's like pinball in slow motion. The AM pastry bakers, on the other hand, are generally more static than their counterparts. Upon their arrival at the bakery, they're presented with one or two large racks of croissants, sticky buns and Danish. These racks are rolled in front of the ovens, the pastry baker formulates the weapons of the trade (egg wash and a pastry brush), and so begins the morning. Pull a tray, apply egg wash, open oven doors, insert trays, garnish pastries, hear buzzer, remove trays, apply egg wash, insert more trays . . .

If the bread baker slowly bounces all morning, the pastry baker does the Twist. Oh, and they duck, too; our bread oven and pastry ovens are fairly snug with each other, and getting burnt by touching a hot tray or catching an 8-foot/2.5-m baker's peel in the forehead is not a great way to start your day. Jackie wore a strapless wedding dress on the day we tied the knot, and the multiple marks on her elbows and biceps were the source of much pride (from the groom) as well as a fair amount of consternation (from the mother of the bride).

While the baking of the croissants happens in the morning, that's just the end point of a process that began 36 hours previously. Dough is mixed and rested overnight, butter is rolled in (a process called "lamination"), the croissants are shaped, then rested a second night, and then baked the next morning. Similar to other products in the bakery, this dough may pass through three or four different baker's hands before they're put out to sell. They're the ultimate expression of technique, patience and teamwork, and we truly feel that there is no better expression of the bakery working in top form than a perfect batch of croissants. It's a wonderful skill to master.

CROISSANT DOUGH

By the way, your croissant will benefit greatly by finding the highest quality butter that you can. Butter with a higher percentage of butter fat, around 83 percent, helps to make a better croissant. There is less water in the butter, and this is beneficial. Plugrá European-Style Butter is a great brand and can be found at specialty grocery stores.

OVERVIEW

- Yield: 5 lbs/2.2 kg laminated croissant dough for croissants or sticky buns
- Desired Dough Temperature: 85°F/30°C
- Mixing Time: 5 minutes
- Bulk Fermentation: 2+ hours
- Refrigeration Time: At least 8 hours
- Lamination Time: 3+ hours
- Resting time before shaping: At least 2 hours

INGREDIENTS

2 lb 12 oz/1.2 kg all-purpose flour

1.5 oz/40 g unsalted butter, softened, plus 1.25 lbs/570 g unsalted butter, chilled to 40°F/4°C in the fridge

4 oz/113 g granulated sugar

0.8 oz/25 g sea salt

1 lb 11oz/765 ml 95°F/35°C water

2.2 oz/63 g milk powder

0.5 oz/15 g instant yeast

Put the flour, sugar and salt into a large mixing bowl. Put the water, milk powder, yeast and butter into another large bowl, swishing it around with your fingers to dissolve the milk powder. Next, dump your dry ingredients on top of the liquid ingredients, and mix by hand for about 30 seconds, until it comes together in a shaggy mass. Once it's come together,

keep mixing for another 30 seconds. No real perceptible dough development will occur, and you don't want to build too much strength here. This dough will be rolled and folded and rolled many more times before it's baked.

Oil a large, rectangular container. A fish tub works best (see page 20), but a deep roasting pan can be just as good. Failing all else, put it in a 9-inch × 13-inch/23 ×33-cm pan and cover with oiled plastic wrap. Let sit in a very warm place for about 2 hours.

Dust the surface with a bit of flour, and push the dough down into the corners of your container, deflating it as much as possible. You want the shape of the dough to be an even rectangle. Refrigerate until ready to laminate, up to 24 hours.

Making the beurrage: whack, whack, whack. Take the chilled butter straight from the refrigerator. Put it on the bottom half of a piece of parchment paper measuring 13 inches × 18 inches/33 × 45 cm. Vigorously hit the block of butter with a rolling pin. It will be loud, so warn bystanders. As the butter flattens, fold it over itself and pound it some more. You want to start to form a rectangle that will fill the bottom half of the parchment. The butter should be cold but pliable. It should not break when bent, and it should also not be mushy. Fold the other half of the parchment over the butter and roll the butter packet into a neat rectangle within the confines of the parchment. The temperature of the butter should be 55°F/13°C before laminating. If it is still too cold after rolling, just allow

it to sit there and warm up. Test it with an instant-read thermometer, and if it gets too warm, pop it in the fridge.

The roll-in: making a book of butter. Take the chilled croissant dough out of the refrigerator. Flour your table generously and tip the dough out onto the table, maintaining the rectangular shape and dimension of the dough, roughly 13 inches × 18 inches/33 × 45 cm. The shorter dimension should be oriented closest to you. Lay the butter on the bottom half of the rectangle of dough, peeling away the parchment paper. Make sure none of the butter is hanging over the edge. If it is, reposition it, and then smooth it out. Next, take the top of the dough and fold it over the top of the butter, pinching the edges of dough together to completely encase the butter. You now have a book of butter. Gently but firmly, with an open hand, press down on the whole book, to make the dough a bit thinner and to press the dough and butter together a bit before rolling it out with the pin.

The first roll-out should be relatively easy, as the dough is still weak. You need to roll it out to 18 inches × 30 inches/45 × 76 cm. Sprinkle the top as well as underneath the dough with flour as needed to prevent sticking, and roll in alternating strokes top to bottom and side to side. Keep the thickness and lines of the rectangle as even as possible. After you have reached your dimensions, brush off all the excess flour with a pastry brush. This is important, because if you do not, the excess flour will gum up the layers during baking when it encounters the steam. This will affect the texture of the final croissant.

Next, perform your first envelope fold by taking the right side of the dough and folding it one-third of the way across. Brush off excess flour on this piece before bringing the left side over on top of it. You can now sprinkle the top lightly with flour. You have your first fold. Place on a parchment-lined sheet pan, dust it with flour, wrap the whole thing in plastic wrap and refrigerate for 45 minutes (not longer, or the butter will get too hard and affect the lamination).

Next it is time for the second fold or turn. Sprinkle some flour down and position the sheet pan so that the seam of the envelope is closest to you and the open part is farthest away. Flip the dough out onto the table. Flip the whole piece over so that that the top becomes the bottom again. Now, roll the dough out to 18 inches × 30 inches/45 × 76 cm again, rolling top to bottom and side to side to stretch the gluten in many different directions. Brush all the surfaces and fold the dough the same way that you did for the first fold. This time the dough will be a bit more resistant, now that the gluten is forming and the dough is cooler. Refrigerate for 45 minutes. Now it's time for the last turn. Perform the steps just as you did for the second fold, but you will notice again that it's a bit harder still to roll it out. Be persistent and roll it out to 18 inches × 30 inches/45 cm × 76 cm. Brush the dough, fold it up and place it back on the sheet pan. This time, rest and chill the dough for a minimum of 2 hours, or as long as overnight. This has the advantage of breaking up the process into 2 days, as well as allowing you to shape and proof the croissants the next morning in time for a breakfast or brunch. (You will probably have to get up early to get them shaped and leave them time to proof and bake, but I guarantee that your guests will appreciate it.) Proceed with one of the recipes that follow. And don't forget to check out the tips on page 169.

PLAIN CROISSANTS

The plain croissant is the most traditional version of this flaky baked good. It is the true measure of properly done lamination, shaping, proofing and baking, as there is nothing such as chocolate or ham and cheese to distract from its perfect simplicity or mask any imperfections. Take this step by step and refer to the photographs as needed.

YIELD: 24 croissants

5 lbs/2.2 kg laminated Croissant Dough (page 147), excess flour brushed off

Egg wash, consisting of 1 beaten egg and a splash of water

Take the laminated dough out of the refrigerator. The dough will be quite cold and stiff, and if it rested overnight, it might be a bit proofed or filled with gas bubbles. This is fine; it means the yeast went into action before the dough cooled back down after all that rolling during the lamination process. Gently pop the bubbles with a sharp object and push the gas out gently. It will be easier to roll if you do this.

Lightly dust your work surface, and flip your dough out onto the table. Dust the surface with just enough flour to prevent your pin from sticking. When you start to roll the dough, do so gently. Don't use lots of force right off the bat, but gently start to nudge the dough with the rolling pin until it starts to give way as it warms and stretches a bit. Once you start to make some purchase, you can start to stretch it a bit more vigorously. Doing so before it's ready could cause the dough to rip and the layers to compact. Roll the dough out to 21 inches × 25 inches/53 × 63 cm. Then, cut that whole rectangle in half at around the 10 ½-inch/26-cm mark. This will leave you with two 10-inch × 25-inch/25 × 63-cm pieces. Gently relax the dough with your hands by lifting it slightly off the table and allowing it to shrink back a little bit. You are now ready to cut and shape the plain croissants.

Starting on the left side of each dough strip and using a bench knife or pizza wheel, trim the edge of the dough by about ½ inch/1 cm. The dough at the very end is somewhat unevenly laminated and doesn't make a nice croissant. Then, working with one strip at a time and starting at the bottom left corner of the strip, make a straight cut upward at about a 30-degree angle to the top of the strip. This means you will have a scrap piece at the left end. Make another cut to meet back down at the bottom of the strip so that the base of the triangle you are creating is about 3 inches/7 cm wide. You have cut your first croissant. You will now make your next identical shape starting back at the base of the first croissant, and you will go back and forth like this until you reach the end of the strip. You should get 12 croissants from each dough strip.

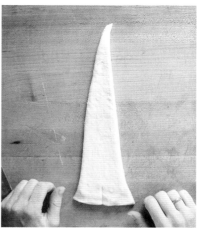

Now, the shape. Take a triangle and orient it so the base of the triangle is closest to you and the point is facing away from you. Make a 1-inch/2.5-cm cut in the middle of the base of the triangle with your bench knife. Then, take your whole triangle in your hands and gently lengthen it by carefully pulling the tail, with your dominant hand, all the way up from the base of the croissant to the pointed end. You just want to gain about 1 inch/2.5 cm in length. Put the croissant back down on the table and grasp the two tabs you have created by making that 1-inch/2.5-cm cut, folding the inside corner of each flap out onto the outside of the triangle. It should rest on top of the outside edge of the dough, not past the dough and onto the table. Gently stretch that part widthwise, then roll the whole thing over itself to get the first part of the roll done. You want a little bit of tension put into that first rollover. Some tucking and downward pressure will help with that. Then, you can roll the croissant up the rest of the way so that the end of the tail is tucked under the middle of the croissant, not sticking out the back end of the croissant. This anchors the whole croissant together so that it does not unroll during proofing or baking. If you wind it too tightly, the appearance will be off and the layers will be impeded in their ability to rise tall and proud. You won't get much of a mohawk ridge on the top tier. Once you have shaped all the croissants, place them on a parchment-lined pan and egg wash them all carefully and lightly, avoiding the cut edges where the lamination is exposed. (If you egg wash those edges, it will seal the laminated layers together and the croissants will not rise properly.) Lightly spray a piece of plastic wrap with pan spray and loosely cover the croissants so that they do not dry out.

Proof the croissants at 74°F/20°C for 2 ½ to 3 hours. You want them to grow to about double in size and take on a warm marshmallowy texture.

Preheat the oven to 375°F/190°C. Egg wash the croissants lightly again just before baking. Bake for 12 minutes, and then turn the trays for even browning and bake for another 12 minutes or so, until a deep reddish brown color is achieved.

ALMOND CROISSANTS

This is one of our favorite items at the bakery. The filling is sweet, moist and rich, and crisp, and melds so perfectly with buttery croissant layers . The yellow cake makes enough for two batches of croissants, so freeze the leftovers!

YIELD: 24 croissants

5 lbs/2.2 kg of laminated croissant dough (page 147), excess flour brushed off

YELLOW CAKE

7.18 oz/204 g all-purpose flour

1 ½ tsp/6 g baking powder

¾ rounded tsp/5 g fine sea salt

3.75 oz/100 g butter, softened

7.8 oz/220 g sugar

2.5 oz/70 g eggs (1 extra-large egg)

½ tsp/2 ml vanilla extract

6.25 oz/190 ml milk

ALMOND FILLING

4 oz almond paste, broken up

3.25 oz/90 g sugar

3.5 oz/100 g eggs

¾ tsp/5 g fine sea salt

0.5 oz/14 ml rum (or bourbon or brandy or whatever dark liquor you like)

4 oz/110 g sliced natural almonds

8.75 oz/250 g yellow cake crumbs

Egg wash, consisting of 1 beaten egg and a splash of water

¾ cup/130 g sliced almonds, for garnish

To make the yellow cake, preheat the oven to 350°F/180°C. Grease a 9-inch/23-cm cake pan and line the bottom with parchment paper. Combine the flour, baking powder and salt and set aside. Cream the butter and sugar until light and fluffy by rapidly beating the butter and sugar together with a rubber spatula or a wooden spoon. This takes some work. Next, add the eggs and vanilla and mix until completely combined. Alternating wet with dry (finishing with dry), add the milk and the dry ingredients to the mixture. Mix it until it is just (but completely) combined.

Pour the batter into the prepared pan and bake until a skewer poked into the middle comes out clean, about 30 minutes. Let cool, then cross-cut the cake to "butterfly" it open. Lay the open sides on a parchment-lined sheet pan, and dry in a 325°F/160°C oven until golden brown, about 20 minutes.

Cool again, and process, grind or crush by hand until a fine cake crumb consistency is reached.

To make the almond filling, put the first five ingredients in your food processor. (Author's Note: Yep, one of the few instances in this book where you need this gadget!) Process until completely smooth. Combine the almonds and crumbs in a large bowl. Add the processed mixture and mix until you have evenly moistened the crumb mixture. The mixture will hold together in a ball when you squeeze it. Refrigerate the filling for up to 4 days until use, but remove the filling from the refrigerator about 30 minutes before using it. It will be more pliable and easier to roll after warming a bit.

Take the chilled dough out of the refrigerator. The dough will be quite cold and stiff, and if it rested overnight, it might be a bit proofed or filled with gas bubbles. This is fine. Gently pop the gas bubbles with a sharp object and push out the gas.

Lightly dust your work surface, and flip your dough out onto the table. Dust the surface with just enough flour to prevent your pin from sticking. When you start to roll the dough, do so gently. Start to nudge the dough

with the rolling pin until it starts to give way as it warms and stretches a bit. Then you can start to stretch it a bit more vigorously. Doing so before it's ready could cause the dough to rip and the layers to compact. Roll the dough out to 21 inches × 25 inches/50 × 60 cm. Then, cut that whole rectangle in half at around the 10 ½-inch/30-cm mark. This will leave you with two 10-inch × 25-inch/25 × 60-cm pieces. Gently relax the dough with your hands by lifting it slightly off the table and allowing it to shrink back a little bit.

Starting on the left side of each dough strip and using a bench knife or pizza wheel, trim the edge of the dough by about ½ inch/1 cm. Then, working with one strip at a time and starting at the bottom left corner of the strip, make a straight cut upward at about a 30-degree angle to the top of the strip. This means you will have a scrap piece at the top left (not the top, just the entire left edge) end. Make another cut to meet back down at the bottom of the strip so that the base of the triangle you are creating is about 3 inches/7 cm wide. You have cut your first croissant. You will now make your next identical shape starting back at the base of the first croissant, and you will go back and forth like this until you reach the end of the strip. You should get 12 croissants from each dough strip.

Now, the shape. Take a triangle and orient it so the base of the triangle is closest to you and the point is facing away from you. Make a 1-inch/2.5-cm cut in the middle of the base of the triangle with your bench knife. Then, take your whole triangle in your hands and gently lengthen it by carefully pulling the tail, with your dominant hand, all the way up from the base of the croissant to the pointed end. You just want to gain about 1 inch/2.5 cm in length.

Take approximately 0.85 ounces/24 g of the filling (you can eyeball after the first few) and form it into a small, flat triangle. Orient this filling on the unrolled croissant triangle to mirror the same shape. Now, grasp the two ears you have created by making that 1-inch/2.5-cm cut, folding the inside corner of each flap out onto the outside of the triangle. It should rest on top of the outside edge of the dough, not past the dough and onto the table. Gently stretch that part widthwise, and roll the dough deliberately up and over the almond filling to get the first part of the roll done. You want a little bit of tension put into that first rollover. Some tucking and downward pressure will help with that. Then, you can roll the croissant up the rest of the way so that the end of the tail is tucked under the middle of the croissant, not sticking out the back end of the croissant. This anchors the whole croissant together so that it does not unroll during proofing or baking. If you wind it too tightly, the appearance will be off and the layers will not rise fully. Once you have shaped all the croissants, place them on parchment-lined sheet pans and egg wash them all carefully and lightly, avoiding the cut edges where the lamination is exposed. Lightly spray a piece of plastic wrap with pan spray and loosely cover the croissants so that they do not dry out.

Proof the croissants at 74°F/20°C for 2 ½ to 3 hours. You want them to grow to about double in size and take on a warm marshmallowy texture.

Preheat the oven to 375°F/190°C. Egg wash the croissants lightly again just before baking as well, and garnish with sliced almonds. Bake for 12 minutes, and then turn the tray for even browning and bake for another 12 minutes or so, until a deep reddish brown color is achieved.

PAIN AU CHOCOLAT

The pain au chocolat is a real breakfast treat. There isn't so much chocolate in each one that you have to feel guilty. Dipped into the foam of a cappuccino, we find it irresistible. You can purchase special chocolate sticks called chocolate batons for making pain au chocolat, which are convenient when rolling up the croissant. You can also use chocolate chips or broken chocolate bars or any other high-quality chocolate that will melt well when wrapped inside the croissant dough. The sticks happen to be convenient for the action of rolling up the croissant.

YIELD: 28 croissants

5 lbs/2.2 kg laminated Croissant Dough (page 147), excess flour brushed off

56 chocolate batons, or 12 oz/ 340 g chocolate chips or chopped chocolate

Egg wash, consisting of 1 beaten egg and a splash of water

Remove the chilled croissant dough from the refrigerator. The dough will be quite cold and stiff, and if it rested overnight, it might be a bit proofed or filled with gas bubbles. This is fine. Gently pop those gas bubbles with a sharp object and push out the gas.

Lightly dust your work surface, and flip your dough out onto the table. Dust the surface with just enough flour to prevent your pin from sticking. When you start to roll the dough, do so gently. Start to nudge the dough with the rolling pin until it starts to give way as it warms and stretches a bit. Then you can start to stretch it a bit more vigorously. Roll the dough out to 21 inches × 25 inches/50 × 60 cm. Then, cut that whole rectangle in half at around the 10 ½-inch/26-cm mark. This will leave you with two 10-inch × 25-inch/25 × 60-cm pieces. Gently relax the dough with your hands by lifting it slightly off the table and allowing it to shrink back a little bit. You are now ready to cut and shape the pain au chocolat, using (if you have) the chocolate batons. They are about 3 inches/7 cm long, so if you place one horizontally at the bottom of the strip farthest to the left for the first cut, you will have a good guideline for how large to cut each rectangle. You need to cut it about ½ inch/1 cm wider than the baton. Each rectangle should be 3 ½ inches to 4 inches/9 to 10 cm long. Make a vertical cut from the bottom of each strip all the way through to the top of each strip. You now have seven long rectangles in each strip. Take the midpoint of the entire strip, which will be around 5 inches/12 cm, and cut across the rectangles in order to create 14 pieces per strip. You now have 14 smaller rectangles, or 28 pieces overall.

Take each rectangle of dough and lay one stick at the bottom of each piece closest to you. Do this for each croissant, then egg wash a 1-inch/2.5-cm band at the top. Roll the croissant from the bottom up, wrapping the first baton in the dough. Put a little tension in that first roll. Take a second baton and lay it on the seam you have created and roll the croissant the rest of the way up. The croissant should sit on top of the seam, with it positioned in the middle of the croissant to anchor it down and seal it. Once you have shaped all the croissants and laid them on a parchment-lined sheet pan, egg wash all the croissants. Lightly spray a piece of plastic wrap with pan spray and loosely cover the croissants so that they do not dry out.

Proof the croissants for 2 ½ to 3 hours at 74°F/20°C. You want them to grow to about double in size and take on a warm marshmallowy texture. Egg wash them just before baking as well.

Preheat the oven to 375°F/190°C. Bake for 12 minutes, and then turn the tray for even browning and bake for another 12 minutes or so, until a deep reddish brown color is achieved.

HAM AND CHEESE CROISSANTS

These croissants are kind of addictive. The saltiness from the ham and the added richness from the cheese combine nicely to create a savory breakfast treat. The addition of black pepper adds a bright spot for your palate to help balance it out.

YIELD: 28 croissants

5 lbs/2.2 kg laminated Croissant Dough (page 147), excess flour brushed off

56 ham batons, approximately 3 in × ¼ in × ¼ in/7 cm × 5 mm × 5 mm (about 1 lb 4 oz/550 g)

1 lb 2 oz/500 g Gruyere cheese, grated

Cracked black pepper (optional)

Egg wash, consisting of 1 beaten egg and a splash of water

¼ cup/40 g sesame seeds (optional)

Remove the chilled croissant dough from the refrigerator. The dough will be quite cold and stiff, and if it rested overnight, it might be a bit proofed or filled with gas bubbles. This is fine. Gently pop those gas bubbles with a sharp object and push out the gas.

Lightly dust your work surface, and flip your dough out onto the table. Dust the surface with just enough flour to prevent your pin from sticking. When you start to roll the dough, do so gently. Start to nudge the dough with the rolling pin until it starts to give way as it warms and stretches a bit. Then you can start to stretch it a bit more vigorously. Doing so before it's ready could cause the dough to rip and the layers to compact. Roll the dough out to 21 inches × 25 inches/50 × 60 cm. Then, cut that whole rectangle in half at around the 10 ½-inch/26-cm mark. This will leave you with two 10-inch × 25-inch/25 × 60-cm pieces. Gently relax the dough with your hands by lifting it slightly off the table and allowing it to shrink back a little bit.

Using a bench knife or a pizza wheel, trim ½ inch/1 cm off the left side of each strip. Each rectangle should be 3 ½ inches to 4 inches/9 to 10-cm long. Make a vertical cut from the bottom of each strip all the way through to the top of each strip. You now have seven long rectangles in each strip. Take the midpoint of the entire strip, which will be around 5 inches/12 cm, and cut across the rectangles in order to create 14 pieces per strip. You now have 14 smaller rectangles, or 28 all together.

Each croissant will get two ham batons and about 0.65 ounces/18 g cheese, or roughly 2 tablespoons. Place one ham baton at the end of the unrolled croissant closest to you. Sprinkle the cheese on top of the croissant (and, if you like, cracked black pepper), leaving approximately ¼ inch/5 mm on either side and about 1 inch/2.5 cm at the top. Egg wash the band at the top.

Roll the croissant from the bottom up, wrapping the first ham baton and almost all of the cheese in your first roll (some of the cheese will fall out, which is okay). After the ham and cheese are completely covered, put your second ham baton snugly against the rolled section, and finish rolling it up over the rest of the ham. Make sure that the finished croissant is sitting directly on its seam anchored in the middle of the croissant. Place them all on parchment-lined sheet trays. Lightly spray pieces of plastic wrap with pan spray and loosely cover the croissants so that they do not dry out.

Proof the croissants for 2 ½ to 3 hours at 74°F/20°C. You want them to grow to about double in size and take on a warm marshmallowy texture. Egg wash them just before baking as well and garnish with sesame seeds, if you like.

Preheat the oven to 375°F/190°C. Bake for 12 minutes, and then turn the tray for even browning and bake for another 12 minutes or so, until a deep reddish brown color is achieved.

DIAMOND DANISH

We call these diamond-shaped croissants Danish, but it's a misnomer, really. This shape is often used when making Danish. We make three basic types of these filled diamond croissants at the bakery: cheese, lemon and jam filled. The jam flavor changes with the seasons.

YIELD: 20 Danish

5 lbs/2.2 kg laminated Croissant Dough (page 147), excess flour brushed off

Filling of choice (recipes follow)

Egg wash, consisting of 1 beaten egg and a splash of water

Take the chilled laminated dough out of the refrigerator. The dough will be quite cold and stiff, and if it rested overnight, it might be a bit proofed or filled with gas bubbles. This is fine. Gently pop those gas bubbles with a sharp object and push out the gas.

Lightly dust your work surface, and flip your dough out onto the table. Dust the surface with just enough flour to prevent your pin from sticking. When you start to roll the dough, do so gently. Start to nudge the dough with the rolling pin until it starts to give way as it warms and stretches a bit. Then you can start to stretch it a bit more vigorously. Doing so before it's ready could cause the dough to rip and the layers to compact. Roll the dough out to 21 inches × 25 inches/50 × 60 cm. Then, cut that whole rectangle in half across the whole piece at around the 10 ½-inch/26-cm mark. This will leave you with two 10-inch × 25-inch/25 × 60-cm pieces. Gently relax the dough with your hands by lifting it slightly off the table and allowing it to shrink back a little bit. You are now ready to shape the Danish.

Using a bench knife or a pizza wheel, trim ½ inch/1 cm off the left side of each strip. Each rectangle should be 4 ½ inches to 5 inches/11 to 12 cm wide. Remember, the dough may shrink when you cut it, so estimate a little high and the dough will settle back to the proper dimension after cutting. Make a vertical cut from the bottom of each strip all the way through to the top of each strip. You now have five long rectangles in each strip. You will now take the midpoint of the entire strip, which will be around 5 inches/12 cm, and cut across the rectangles in order to create 10 squares per strip. It's important that they be square, more so than that the exact 5-inch × 5-inch/12 × 12-cm dimension be achieved, though they should be close to that. Trim the pieces as needed to make sure they will be square.

Take each square and fold it in half diagonally to form a triangle. Then, with your bench knife make a cut through the seam almost to the end of the point of the triangle. This cut should be about ½ inch/1 cm wide. Do not cut all the way through the tip! Leave about ¼ inch/5 mm. Do the same on the other side. Now, unfold the triangle back into a square. Take each of the opposite points and cross them over each other. There will be a well in the center and two points at the top and bottom.

Put the shapes on a parchment-lined sheet pan, egg wash the surfaces, but not inside the well, and then fill. You will be able to fit about 1 tablespoon/20 g of filling in the well. If the jam is loose, don't fill them until they are proofed and ready to go in the oven or the jam will start to leak out. You will have to prod your way into the well a little bit after it is proofed, but they will rebound just fine in the oven. If the jam is good and stiff, go ahead and fill them before proofing. Lightly spray a piece of plastic wrap with pan spray and loosely cover the croissants so that they do not dry out.

Proof the Danish for 2 to 2 ½ hours at 74°F/20°C. You want them to grow to about double in size and take on a warm marshmallowy texture. These proof faster than all the other shapes because they are less hindered by their shaping.

Preheat the oven to 375°F/190°C. Bake the Danish for 12 minutes, then turn the pan for even browning and bake for another 12 to 15 minutes, until a deep reddish brown color is achieved. Some of the leaking filling may burn on the parchment, but this can easily be separated from the croissant when still warm or peeled off when cooler.

CHEESE DANISH FILLING

If you have filling left over, store it in the refrigerator for up to 1 week in an airtight container. It makes a great spread for toast, muffins and bagels.

YIELD: 20 oz/570 g

- **18 oz/510 g cream cheese, softened**
- **2 oz/60 g confectioners' sugar**
- **½ tsp/2 g grated orange zest**

Using a rubber spatula or a countertop mixer with paddle attachment (booooo), mix and fold the cream cheese until smooth. Add confectioners' sugar and orange zest, and mix until well combined. *C'est finis.* Refrigerate until ready to use, or for up to 1 week.

LEMON CURD FILLING

Lemon curd is great for so many things. You can use it in a tart filling, to flavor whipped cream, simply spread it on a piece of toast, or even stir it into yogurt or ice cream! Any leftovers can be stored in the refrigerator in an airtight container for about 1 week.

YIELD: 24 oz/680 g

10.5 oz/300 g granulated sugar

2 ½ tsp/7 g grated lemon zest

4.5 oz/130 g egg yolks

5.75 oz/160 ml lemon juice

2 pinches fine sea salt

3.5 oz/100 g unsalted butter, cubed and softened

Rub the sugar and zest together in a 2-quart/2-L heavy-bottom stainless steel pot until fragrant and moist. Add the egg yolks to the sugar-zest mixture and whisk until combined. Add the lemon juice, salt and butter. Cook on medium-low heat, stirring constantly with a rubber spatula and taking care to drag the spatula along the bottom to avoid scorching or scrambling your eggs. Cook until the butter is melted and the mixture is steaming. Never boil or even simmer the mixture, or you'll coagulate and scramble the eggs. The curd is done when it coats the back of a spoon and leaves a trace when you run your finger along the spoon's covered surface, about 10 minutes. If you want to use a thermometer, it's done when it reaches 175°F/80°C.

Strain the curd through a fine-mesh strainer into a bowl and cover the surface immediately with plastic wrap to prevent the curd from forming a skin. Refrigerate it immediately. After cooling completely, remove the plastic wrap and use it immediately or store in a covered container for up to 2 weeks. The curd will have stiffened at this point, and will sit nicely in your Danish.

CONCORD GRAPE JAM FILLING

Concord grapes are known for their beautiful, deep purple color and their robust, slightly pungent flavor. They have thick skins and difficult-to-remove seeds, making them somewhat of an acquired taste when eaten whole, but they really are a short-lived treat in the areas where they grow. They make the truly classic grape jam. There is a lot of pectin in the skins, so no added pectin is needed to set it.

2 quarts/2 L stemmed grapes (3 dry quarts grapes equals about 2 quarts stemmed grapes)

Water as needed

5 cups/960 g granulated sugar

Separate the skins from the pulp by slipping the green innards out of the skins with your fingers.

Put the pulp—seeds and all—in a heavy stainless steel pot, and put the skins in another pot. Cook the skins gently for 15 to 20 minutes with just enough water to keep them from scorching (about ½ cup/120 ml to start, adding more as needed). Remove them from the heat and set them aside. Bring the pulp to a boil and cook until the grape pulp takes on a whitish hue. Strain the seeds out by pushing the pulp through a fine-mesh sieve.

Combine the pulp, skins and sugar in a pot and slowly heat, stirring to dissolve the sugar. Boil rapidly for about 10 minutes to reach a gelling point of 216°F/102°C. Remove from the heat. Skim off the foam. Cool and refrigerate in an airtight container for several months.

KUMQUAT MARMALADE FILLING

Kumquats are not available year-round in New England. Around December, we order our first supply of them and start stockpiling until they are no longer available. Kumquats are unique in that you can eat the entire fruit—skin, seeds and all. They take a bit of extra work to slice and seed, but they give this marmalade a little more texture as well as a bit of a fruitier profile, as opposed to straight-up orange marmalade.

2 cups/360 g seeded, sliced kumquats

1 ½ cups/130 g chopped orange flesh (about 2 medium oranges)

1 ½ cups/130 g thinly sliced orange peel (about 2 medium oranges)

1 ½ quarts (40 oz)/1.5 L water

⅓ cup/80 ml lemon juice

Granulated sugar as needed

Slice the kumquats into thin rounds, getting four or five slices per kumquat. Remove the seeds by scraping them out with a paring knife.

Add the kumquats, orange flesh and orange peel strips to a heavy stainless steel pot, and add the water and lemon juice. Cover and refrigerate for 12 to 18 hours.

Bring to a boil and simmer until the peel is tender and most of the water has cooked away, 15 to 20 minutes.

Measure the pulp, skins and liquid into a measuring pitcher. For every cup of the mixture, add 1 cup/190 g sugar. Return it all to the pot and stir to dissolve. Return the pot to the stove along with a candy thermometer and cook until you reach 220°F/104°C. Cook the mixture at this temperature for about 3 minutes. Watch the temperature, color and aroma of the marmalade. You don't want to scorch it.

Skim the foam from the surface of the marmalade and cool in the refrigerator. Store in an airtight container in the refrigerator for several months.

RASPBERRY JAM FILLING

Picking raspberries is not a task to be undertaken if you are in a rush, but some relaxing time spent in a raspberry patch is well worth it on a summer day. You must be careful with this delicate fruit when picking them, and watch out for the thorns! The addition of lemon zest is what makes this jam sing.

2 quarts/2 L raspberries

⅓ cup/80 ml water

1 tbsp/15 ml lemon juice

1 tbsp/9 g lemon zest

1 (1.75 oz/50 g) package pectin, such as Ball® Original Fruit Pectin

42 oz/1 kg granulated sugar

Combine the first five ingredients in the pot. Stir and bring to a boil over high heat, making sure to watch carefully to prevent scorching. Add the sugar and stir to dissolve the sugar.

Then, bring it all back to a rolling boil that cannot be stirred down. Boil like that for 1 minute. Skim the scum and store the jam in an airtight container in the refrigerator for several months.

TIPS FOR LAMINATING AND SHAPING CROISSANTS

1. When rolling out your dough while laminating, make sure to not use too much heavy-handed downward pressure, but rather pull and stretch the dough with the pin to lengthen and thin it out. Too much downward pressure will lead to damaged, compacted layers that will not rise properly and will not yield a flaky croissant.

2. While you are laminating, if your butter breaks into a scaly texture that you can see underneath the layer of dough, the temperature of your butter was either too high or too low. Low-quality butter can also create this issue. All is not lost, but it may affect the final appearance; the croissants might look mottled. A little of the butter might leak out and the flakiness may be compromised a bit, as the hard butter could break through some of the layers. Don't scrap it, though. Keep going. Sometimes this smoothes out over the course of the laminating process, and if you do everything else right, your croissants will still be vastly superior to anything you can get at your local chain coffee shop.

3. If you do not anchor your seams correctly, the croissants will unroll. You should not see the open cut end of the croissant from the other side of the croissant when it's resting on the sheet pan. If you do, it's going to unroll like a sleeping bag during proofing and certainly during baking.

4. If your croissants are leaking a lot of butter during the baking process, the oven temperature might not have been high enough or your croissants were quite underproofed.

STICKY BUNS

These sticky buns are one of the items that made our bakery popular right off the bat. It is so hard to deny the addictive qualities of cinnamon and brown sugar combined with flaky, buttery dough. When they are warm and paired with a great cup of coffee, you have it made. You can make the sticky bun sugar as dark or light as you want, depending on the type of molasses you use (for example, blackstrap is quite dark and smoky; golden molasses is more mild).

YIELD: 16 buns

5 lbs/2.2 kg laminated Croissant Dough (page 147), excess flour brushed off

3 lb/1.5 kg granulated sugar

2.4 oz/70 g molasses

1 oz/30 g ground cinnamon

8 oz/230 g walnut or pecan pieces (optional)

Put the sugar in a bowl and pour the molasses over it. Mix it in with your hands until all the sugar is moist and coated. Add the cinnamon and do the same thing. Brown sugar dries out quickly if not covered, so store in an airtight container.

Roll and cut the dough into two 10-inch × 25-inch/25 × 60-cm dough strips as directed on page 150. Cover each strip with 1 pound 8 ounce/ 700 g of the sugar mixture, spreading it evenly almost to the edges. Then, working with one piece at a time and starting on the left side, roll the dough halfway up to the top of the strip with your fingers. You want to put a bit of tension into this first windup. Continue rolling it up all the way to the top of the strip. You do not need to seal the edge. Using your bench knife or a sharp, serrated bread knife, cut eight 4-inch/10-cm sticky buns from each roll.

Spray two 12-cup/4-g muffin pans well with cooking spray and then place them on parchment-lined sheet pans. Fill each cup with a layer of chopped walnuts or pecans if you want sticky buns "with," and then place either cut end of the sticky bun into the cup. Fill each tray with eight buns each. Not filling all 12 cups will allow for easier, more even baking. You will see the lovely brown sugar spiral on top after placing them in the pans.

At this point you could refrigerate the trays of buns, remove them from the fridge in the morning, proof them for 45 minutes and then bake them. You would have fresh, warm sticky buns for breakfast. To bake them right away, allow them to proof for 45 minutes (at 74°F/20°C).

Preheat the oven to 375°F/190°C. Bake the sticky buns for 45 to 50 minutes, rotating the pans after 25 minutes top to bottom. The buns in the middle will take the longest to bake and will be the mostly likely to be underbaked if you take them out too soon. If they are underbaked, they will collapse during the cooling process. The middle buns will appear paler than the outer ones no matter what, but you want to avoid their looking very doughy when you take them out.

Once you remove them from the oven, put the whole sheet pan down on the counter. Pick up the muffin tin and quickly invert it onto the parchment-lined sheet pan. (Putting down a clean piece of parchment on top of the greasy piece makes for a cleaner presentation.) If there is excess sugar in the muffin tin, tip it over and drain it onto the buns. Try to cool a bit before eating or else you will burn the heck out of your mouth!

BREAD PUDDING

Bread pudding is one of our favorite things to make at the bakery, and we've been making it since day one. Bread puddings are simple; they can be adapted to whatever fruits or flavors are in season (or whichever ones you have on hand); they taste great hot, cold or room temperature; and they use up extra croissant scraps or leftovers from the end of that inevitable slow day. There's not a lot of science to it. You need a bread product to soak up your custard, and you need enough custard to soak into the bread. That's pretty much it. Make sure to use stale bread (or stale it yourself by leaving it on your counter for a few hours), as fresh bread tends to fall apart when absorbing the liquid. It will still be tasty made with fresh bread, but maybe a little less pleasing texturally, and certainly harder to slice into nice wedges for a plated dessert. These recipes that we serve at the bakery should be viewed as solid offerings as well as jumping-off points. Once you get the idea of how to assemble bread pudding, you'll be off and running with your own unique flavor combinations.

CARAMEL-BOURBON-PECAN BREAD PUDDING

Bourbon, caramel and pecans are naturals together. There's not much more to it than that. The bourbon and caramel help to moisten the bread and provide the highlights for this bread pudding. Extra caramel sauce can be stored at room temperature in an airtight container for a couple of weeks and up to 1 month in the refrigerator. Reheat and use whenever your sweet tooth calls.

YIELD: One 5-in × 9-in/12 × 23-cm pan or one 7-in/18-cm round paper mold

CARAMEL

10.5 oz/300 g sugar

1.5 oz/40 ml water

1.75 oz/50 ml agave nectar or corn syrup

¾ cup/180 ml heavy cream

3 oz/85 g butter

3 large eggs

8 oz/240 ml whole milk

8 oz/240 ml half-and-half

¼ cup/60 ml bourbon

¼ cup/50 g sugar

1 tbsp/15 ml pure vanilla extract

1 lb/450 g stale croissant, brioche, challah or other bread, cut into 1"/2.5-cm dice

4 oz/110 g pecans, toasted

To make the caramel, combine the sugar, water and agave in a very clean, heavy-bottom stainless steel pot. Make sure any utensils you use are very clean, as impurities in your caramel can cause it to crystallize. Warm over medium heat, stirring to dissolve the sugar. Once dissolved, turn the heat to high. Boil until a dark amber color is achieved, periodically washing down the sides of the pot with a pastry brush dipped in water to dissolve any sugar crystallizing.

Carefully add the cream. (Look out for lots of steam! Don't get burned—wear an over mitt if you have one.) Once the bubbling has subsided, add the butter and stir until melted.

Return the caramel to medium heat, and simmer for another 5 minutes to thicken. Cool and refrigerate for long-term storage.

Whisk the eggs, milk, half-and-half, bourbon, sugar and vanilla in a large bowl until combined and smooth. Add the bread and pecans to the bowl, and toss it with your hands or a spoon until all the bread is coated with the custard. Let it sit for at least 30 minutes and up to 1 hour, stirring occasionally.

Preheat the oven to 375°F/190°C. Put half of the bread and custard mixture in your greased pan or mold, gently pressing down to create a mostly flat surface. Spread 2 ounces/60 g (about ¼ cup) caramel on the surface, and top with the remaining bread and custard mixture.

Bake until golden brown and firm when pressed, about 45 minutes. After the bread pudding has cooled down a bit, top with more caramel. Serve with even more caramel if so desired. Caramel, caramel, caramel.

CHOCOLATE-PECAN BREAD PUDDING WITH CHOCOLATE SAUCE

This recipe was one of the first two bread puddings we served at A&J King. This one was chosen specifically so that we could not only use leftover croissants, but leftover Pain au Chocolat (page 156) as well. We certainly had leftovers in those days! Speaking of which, store any leftover chocolate sauce in the refrigerator in an airtight container for 2 weeks. Reheat and use on whatever you like: on ice cream, in your coffee, drizzled over some strawberries.

YIELD: One 5-in × 9-in/12 × 23-cm pan or one 7-in/18-cm round paper mold

3 large eggs

8 oz/240 ml whole milk

8 oz/240 ml half-and-half

¼ cup/50 g sugar

2 tbsp/30 ml pure vanilla extract

1 lb/450 g stale croissant, brioche, challah or other bread, cut into 1"/2.5-cm dice

4 oz/110 g pecan pieces, toasted

5 oz/140 g semisweet chocolate chunks (or bittersweet if you prefer)

CHOCOLATE SAUCE

8 oz/240 ml half-and-half

1.5 lb/700 g semisweet chocolate chunks (you can use darker or lighter chocolate to suit your preference)

Whisk the eggs, milk, half-and-half, sugar and vanilla in a large bowl until combined and smooth.

Add the bread and pecans to the bowl, and toss it with your hands or a spoon until all the bread is coated with the custard. Let sit for at least 30 minutes, or up to 1 hour, stirring occasionally.

Preheat the oven to 375°F/190°C. Put half of the bread and custard mixture in your greased pan or mold, gently pressing down to create a somewhat flat surface. Sprinkle with the chocolate chunks in an even layer. Add the rest of the bread and custard mixture, and press down again.

Bake until golden brown and firm when pressed, about 45 minutes.

While the bread pudding is cooling, make the chocolate sauce: Bring the half-and-half to a simmer and pour it over the chocolate chunks. Whisk until all the chocolate is melted and smooth.

Cool the sauce down a little bit, about 30 minutes, and then drizzle it over the whole bread pudding before cutting. Refrigerate any leftovers for 2 weeks; reheat as needed.

BLUEBERRY-LEMON BREAD PUDDING

We prefer to eat this not-too-sweet pudding on the cool side, with a spoonful of blueberry jam. The lemon gives the custard a crisp finish and is the perfect ending to a summer dinner outside, be it on the porch or picnic blanket. Or out of the fridge with a cold beer. We're serious.

YIELD: One 5-in × 9-in/12 × 23-cm pan or one 7-in/18-cm round paper mold

1 tbsp/9 g lemon zest

½ cup/100 g sugar

3 large eggs

8 oz/240 ml whole milk

8 oz/240 ml half-and-half

1 lb/450 g stale croissant, brioche, challah or other bread, cut into 1"/2.5-cm dice

7 oz/200 g fresh blueberries

Confectioners' sugar, for dusting

In a large bowl, rub the lemon zest into the sugar to release the lemon oil. Add the eggs, milk and half-and-half and whisk until combined and smooth.

Next, add the bread and blueberries to bowl, and toss with your hands or spoon until all the bread is coated with the custard. Let sit for at least 30 minutes or up to 1 hour, stirring occasionally.

Preheat the oven to 375°F/190°C. Put all of the bread and custard mixture into the greased pan or paper mold. Bake until golden brown and firm when pressed, about 45 minutes.

When cooled, dust with confectioners' sugar.

CINNAMON-APPLE-MASCARPONE BREAD PUDDING

I made this recipe for Andy's birthday, which falls near Labor Day. While it is still summer, you can actually get local apples here in the Northeast at that time of year. Some early apples are available as early as late August.

Pro tip: Prepare the apples the day before your party.

Bonus Pro Tip: When you're finished searing the apples and have a pan of melted butter and brown sugar, toss in some brandy, flame it and pour it over ice cream for a treat.

YIELD: One 5-in x 9-in/12 × 23-cm pan or one 7-in/18-cm round paper mold

3 large eggs

8 oz/240 ml whole milk

8 oz/240 ml half-and-half

¾ cup/140 g granulated sugar

1 ½ tsp/4 g ground cinnamon

1 lb/450 g stale croissant, brioche, challah or other enriched dough, 1"/2.5-cm dice

2 Cortland apples or other baking apples

1 oz/30 g unsalted butter

⅓ cup/70 g brown sugar

4 oz/100 g mascarpone cheese

¼ cup/60 ml pure maple syrup

Whisk the eggs, milk, half-and-half, sugar and cinnamon in a large bowl until combined and smooth. Add the bread, and toss it with your hands or spoon until all the bread is coated with the custard. Let it sit for at least 30 minutes (but no longer than 1 hour), stirring occasionally.

While the bread is soaking, prepare the apples (or this can be done up to 1 day in advance). Peel the apples and slice into ½-inch/1-cm slices. Melt the butter in a sauté pan along with the brown sugar over medium heat. Stir until combined. Add the apples and toss to coat completely. Cook until softened and slightly caramelized.

Preheat the oven to 375°F/190°C. Put half the soaked bread into your greased pan or mold. Layer all the apples on top of this first layer of bread. Scoop out the mascarpone cheese into five mounds and place them on top of the apples, evenly spaced. Then, fill with the remainder of the soaked bread. Gently press down on the top to compact it all together slightly.

Bake until golden brown and firm when pressed, about 45 minutes. While still warm, drizzle the top with the maple syrup.

WHITE CHOCOLATE-CHERRY BREAD PUDDING

When the local fruits are scarce as winter crashes down on the Northeast, we make this recipe for customers to serve on their holiday tables. Grab real block white chocolate from a high-end market, as the chips in the baking section are never quite the real deal and don't melt well.

YIELD: One 5-in × 9-in/12 × 23-cm pan or one 7-in/18-cm round paper mold

3 large eggs

8 oz/240 ml whole milk

8 oz/240 ml half-and-half

¼ cup/50 g sugar

1 tbsp/15 ml pure vanilla extract

1 tsp/5 ml almond extract

1 lb/450 g stale croissant, brioche, challah or other bread, cut into 1"/2.5-cm dice

4 oz/110 g dried cherries, rehydrated in hot water for at least 15 minutes and then drained

7 oz/200 g white chocolate chunks

2 oz/50 g sliced almonds

Whisk the eggs, milk, half-and-half, sugar, vanilla extract and almond extract in a large bowl until combined and smooth.

Add the bread and drained cherries to the bowl, and toss with your hands or a spoon until all the bread is coated with the custard. Let it sit for at least 30 minutes (but no longer than 1 hour), stirring occasionally.

Preheat the oven to 375°F/190°C. Put half of the bread and custard mixture in your greased pan or mold, gently pressing down to create a mostly flat surface. Sprinkle with 5 ounces/140 g of the white chocolate chunks in an even layer. Add the rest of the bread and custard mixture, and press down again.

Bake until golden brown and firm when pressed, about 45 minutes. While the bread pudding is baking, spread the almonds on a sheet pan and toast them for 5 to 10 minutes, just until they take on a touch of color. While the bread pudding is cooling, melt the remaining 2 ounces/50 g white chocolate chunks in a double boiler or in the microwave and drizzle over the top of the pudding. Sprinkle with the toasted almonds.

SPICED PUMPKIN BREAD PUDDING WITH MAPLE GLAZE

We'd roast and bake with pumpkins year-round if we could. While most folks associate its flavor with the spices that generally accompany it (this recipe included), roasted pumpkin adds a sweet moistness to everything that incorporates it. You could use canned pumpkin, but please don't. We'll know.

YIELD: One 5-in × 9-in/12 × 23-cm pan or one 7-in/18-cm round paper mold

3 large eggs

7 oz/200 ml whole milk

7 oz/200 ml half-and-half

⅔ cup/130 g granulated sugar

6 oz/175 g roasted pureed pumpkin (see Note)

1 ¼ tsp/3 g ground cinnamon

¾ tsp/1.5 g ground allspice

¼ tsp/0.5 g ground nutmeg

1 lb/450 g stale croissant, brioche, challah or other bread, cut into 1"/2.5-cm dice

MAPLE GLAZE

6.5 oz/180 g confectioners' sugar

2 oz/50 g maple sugar

2 oz/60 ml half-and-half

Whisk the eggs, milk, half-and-half, sugar, pumpkin puree and spices in a large bowl until combined and smooth.

Add the bread, and toss with your hands or spoon until all the bread is coated with the custard. Let it sit for at least 30 minutes or up to 1 hour, stirring occasionally.

Preheat the oven to 375°F/190°C. Put all of the bread and custard mixture into the greased pan or paper mold. Bake until golden brown and firm when pressed, about 45 minutes.

To make the glaze, whisk all of the ingredients together until smooth and lump-free.

When cooled, drizzle the pudding with the glaze.

NOTE: For the roasted pumpkin, cut a small sugar pumpkin in half. Remove the strings and seeds. Bake in a 400°F/200°C oven until the flesh is tender and a knife inserted moves through easily, about 1 hour. Cool the pumpkin and peel the skin off. Purée the pumpkin and refrigerate until you are ready to use it.

THE PM PASTRY BAKER

CRUSTS, SEASONAL SWEETS AND SAVORY TARTS

Later in the day, after the rush of the morning bake has passed, we have many other bakers who come in to perform various tasks. One of those tasks is to do all the makeup for the seasonal tarts that we have available each day. While the arm burns are a little less frequent during this shift, there are still plenty of other important things to do. Each tart is treated differently depending on the components. This is what keeps us on our toes when testing day rolls around; we are not only putting flavor combinations together, but what we create also has to work in terms of texture and function. If two of the components can't be placed harmoniously in the crust, it's not going to work.

We love seeing how we can take what the season brings us and turn it into an expression of our taste and aesthetic here at the bakery. It's what helps to keep us excited and flexible within the somewhat rigid system of formulae and detail that comes with working in a bakery.

ANDY'S TRIP TO THE FARM

While Jackie had promised that I would be able to get them at the farm, I couldn't find one single sugar pumpkin. The big wooden crate that usually housed the pile of orange globes still had the sign up, but all that it contained were broken stems and dried field dirt. I waved to get the attention of two fellows leaning behind the retail counter, and I asked if there were any pumpkins left, because showing up at the bakery empty-handed was not an option. I got a surprisingly descriptive sharp nod to the back door, which opened up onto a field of beautiful, ripe pumpkins, wet with the cold fall rain and ready for the picking. I thought of the classic French chef perusing the local farmers markets, looking for the perfect vegetables for the night's tasting menus, something I always thought was a bit of a show for the television crews. But there I was, slogging through the mud and vines, searching for the perfect pumpkins to take back to the bakery, and I was practically giddy. It's rare that you get something so fresh that you've released it from the earth minutes before it goes into the oven, but that's the crux of what makes us so passionate about seasonal pastry.

Not all trips to the farm are that soggy, mind you. Sunburns can be had in strawberry fields, and cider doughnuts generally accompany us on the way home from any of Massachusetts' plentiful fruit orchards. But there's one constant: When your day of pastry baking starts with a trip to the local farm, and then you trek farther out into the fields to scrabble around for the best-looking fruit you can find, you're going to have a good day in the kitchen.

LAZY BAKER'S PUFF PASTRY DOUGH

Making real puff pastry is a beautiful thing, with all of those flaky layers, brittle and shattering. It's also a huge time commitment, so we like to use this adaptation of dough that we first came across in one of our much-loved King Arthur baking books. This dough is flaky and extremely rich and tender due to the high percentage of butter and the sour cream. Its acidity helps tenderize the dough and the fat adds more richness. Lastly, the baking powder helps to give the layers their needed puff in this short cut version of this pastry classic. We have created many bakery favorites using this versatile recipe.

YIELD: Six 7-in/18-cm rounds for 5-in/12-cm tartlets

11 oz/300 g all-purpose flour

1 scant tsp/3 g baking powder

¾ tsp/5 g fine sea salt

13 oz/370 g cold unsalted butter

6.5 oz/180 g cold sour cream

Place the flour, baking powder and salt into a container that will easily fit in your freezer. Chill the mixture for 30 minutes or overnight. You can't chill it for too long.

In the meantime, cube your butter into about ½-inch/1-cm cubes. Keep chilled in the refrigerator.

Once the flour has chilled sufficiently, put it in a bowl and add the chilled butter. Rub the butter through the flour to break it up and incorporate it. Keep at it until the butter is broken down but you still see chunks of butter. The chunks should be a little larger than large peas. You want the butter to stay in large chunks in order to create a flaky crust.

Add the sour cream to the dry ingredients and mix by hand. Form a shaggy mass of dough just until all of the moisture is absorbed and there are no dry spots. You do not want to overwork it so much that you break down the butter completely.

Turn the dough out onto a floured counter and form into a rough rectangle. Roll the dough out until it becomes a larger 6-inch × 16-inch/15 × 40-cm rectangle. Sprinkle the surface of the dough with flour, grab the left hand side of the rectangle and place one-third of the surface into the middle. Then, do the same with the right side, completely overlapping the left side with this "envelope fold." Rotate the dough 90 degrees. Roll out to another 6-inch × 16-inch/15 × 40-cm rectangle, then lightly flour and fold the dough again as before.

Take this packet of dough, place it on a sheet pan and wrap in plastic wrap. Chill the dough for 1 hour to relax before using, or wrap tightly with plastic wrap and freeze.

NOTE: After cutting out your rounds for the various recipes, you can chill, rest and roll out the scraps after about 2 hours in the fridge; there will be enough left for two 7-inch/18-cm circles. If you don't want to take the time to make the extra circles, just turn scraps into cookies (see page 223).

Rolling Lazy Bakers Puff Pastry into flan rings. This method is used often in the related recipes.

BAKING STONES: THEY'RE NOT JUST FOR BREAD ANYMORE

At the bakery, most of our pastries are baked in your standard commercial convection oven. However, when your products are filled with fresh, juice-laden, local fruits, you need an extra shot of heat on the crust to keep it from getting soggy. This is where the baking stone comes in handy. The retained heat that gives bread such strong oven spring also will seal the bottom of the Lazy Baker's Puff Pastry, as well as the 3-2-1 Pie Dough before those juices start flowing—not to mention that all-over beautiful golden brown crust that Jackie requires for her pies and tarts.

3-2-1 PIE DOUGH

This recipe is perfect because it's incredibly easy to remember, amazingly easy to produce and infinitely applicable to treats both sweet and savory. It has saved our butts a few times when we had excess fruit at the end of a summer day.

Here's where the "3-2-1" part fits in: By weight, this dough is three parts flour, two parts butter and one part ice water. Plus, throw in a teaspoon/7 g of fine sea salt for every double-crust pie you're baking. That's it. Now you can make any quantity you need.

YIELD: Enough pastry for 1 standard two-crust pie

12 oz/340 g chilled all-purpose flour

1 tsp/7 g fine sea salt

8 oz/250 g cold unsalted butter, cut into medium dice

4 oz/110 ml ice water

Combine the cold flour, salt and cold butter in a large bowl. Using your fingers, begin to pinch and combine the butter and flour, making sure not to hold the butter in your hands too long. Keep working the flour and butter between your fingers until the largest pieces of butter are no smaller than peas. The key is to keep this mixture as cold as possible, and if you feel that it is warming up too much, you can refrigerate it.

Add the ice water to the flour-butter mixture, and toss together with your fingers, eventually pressing it together with your hands. You want a dough to form with no dry patches or crumbly parts, but you do not want to overwork it so much that you break down the butter completely. Otherwise, you will lose flakiness and your dough will become tougher. You want to see streaks of butter running through the dough.

Divide the dough into two equal pieces and wrap them in plastic wrap. Chill for at least 1 hour before proceeding or overnight. You could also freeze it at this point for future use.

RHUBARB-GINGER TARTS WITH OAT TOPPING

Andy loves rhubarb! Those who really love it prefer it straight up, rather than in the traditional favorite, strawberry-rhubarb pie. It's got a sourness that is a great foil to the rich pastry crust and the sugar. The ginger adds a nice accent to the whole combination. Both have a slightly pungent quality that makes this tart a hit with rhubarb lovers. I even had a customer tell me that he was so happy to see rhubarb on its own!

YIELD: Six 5-in/12-cm tartlets

1 recipe Lazy Baker's Puff Pastry Dough (page 185)

FILLING

1 lb 2 oz/500 g rhubarb

5.75 oz/160 g granulated sugar

2.25 oz/60 g finely diced crystallized ginger

1 ½ tbsp/14 g cornstarch

OAT TOPPING

3.5 oz/100 g rolled oats

3.5 oz/100 g all-purpose flour

1.7 oz/48 g granulated sugar

¼ tsp/2 g fine sea salt

½ tsp/1 g ground cinnamon

3.5 oz/100 g unsalted butter, melted

Egg wash, consisting of 1 beaten egg and a splash of water

To make the crust, spray six 5-inch/12-cm flan rings with cooking spray. Roll out your dough to about 14 inches × 27 inches/35 × 70 cm, cut out six 7-inch/18-cm circles and place them in the flan rings. Lifting up around the entire perimeter of the disk, "settle" the dough into the corners of the rings. Then, working from the outside in, roll the overlapping dough until you can press the roll into the side of the flan rings, creating a thicker outer crust with a thin bottom. Chill in the refrigerator until ready to use.

For the filling, clean and trim the ends of the rhubarb. If the pieces are especially fat, slice them lengthwise in half. Then, chop it into medium dice. Place in a large bowl and add the sugar, crystallized ginger and cornstarch. Allow to macerate for 30 minutes. Meanwhile, make the oat topping.

To make the oat topping, combine all of the dry ingredients in a bowl. Pour the melted butter over the dry ingredients and mix everything together with your fingers until the mixture is completely moist. Set aside at room temperature until ready to use. (This can be made ahead and refrigerated for at least 1 week in an airtight container.)

ASSEMBLING THE TARTLETS

Preheat your oven to 450°F/230°C, with the baking stone in place and the oven rack in the middle position.

Take the chilled tart dough set into its rings and egg wash the rims. With a slotted spoon and letting excess liquid drain away, fill each tart just with the rhubarb filling to below the edge of the shell. If you keep all that liquid in the tart shell, it will bubble over and create a burnt mess in the oven. Use up all the fruit among the six shells.

Place the sheet pan directly on the baking stone and bake for 15 minutes. Remove the tarts from the oven and add the oat topping to cover the rhubarb. Return the tarts to the oven, this time on the rack rather than on the baking stone. Bake for another 25 to 30 minutes. Use a spatula to lift the edge of one of the tarts and peek beneath to confirm that the bottoms are a deep golden brown color; this will be the final sign that the tarts are fully cooked. If the top is browning too fast, cover the whole lot with a sheet of aluminum foil.

Remove from the oven and immediately remove the rings, or else they will stick to the tarts as they cool. Allow to cool for 15 minutes on a rack before handling or eating.

STRAWBERRY-ALMOND CREAM TARTS

The fruit is on full display here, so you won't get away with this if you're using February strawberries from the grocery store. Go out to the farm and pick them yourself; that's the essence of simplicity that we love to present. Toasted almonds give the tart some added texture and another flavor highlight for the palate as well. The range given for the strawberries is due to their varying sizes. Local ones are often on the smaller side, and so it will take sometimes as many as seven halves to cover the surface of each tart.

YIELD: Eight 4-in/10-cm tartlets

CRUST

1.2 oz/34 g almond meal

8.6 oz/243 g flour

¼ tsp/2 g fine sea salt

5.2 oz/147 g unsalted butter

4 oz/100 g granulated sugar

1 oz/30 g egg yolks

1 egg white, lightly beaten

PASTRY CREAM

13.9 oz/411 g half-and-half

2.3 oz/65 g granulated sugar, plus 0.8 oz/22 g sugar

Pinch of fine sea salt

½ vanilla bean, split and scraped

2.6 oz/70 g egg yolks

0.8 oz/22 g cornstarch

1.75 oz/50 g unsalted butter, cubed, softened

1 ½ cups/255 g sliced toasted almonds

24 to 48 strawberries, hulled

8 sprigs fresh mint (optional)

To make the crust, combine the almond meal, flour and salt in a bowl. In another bowl, combine the soft butter with the sugar. Mix it together with a wooden spoon or rubber spatula until no lumps are present and a smooth paste has formed. Add the egg yolks and mix to combine. Then, add all the dry ingredients and stir until a slightly dry dough is formed. Chill for 30 minutes before rolling out. Don't let it get too cold, or it will crack and crumble.

Roll the dough out to about a ⅛-inch/3-mm thickness. Cut eight circles with a 4 ½-inch or 5-inch/11 or 12-cm cutter. Press them into the tart pans and trim any excess. Chill for at least 30 minutes, or overnight.

Preheat your oven to 375°F/190°C. Prick the bottoms of the tarts with a fork. Place aluminum foil or parchment paper in the cavity and fill it with dried beans or rice. Bake for 20 minutes, and then remove the beans. Bake for another 5 to 7 minutes, until golden brown and completely dried out. Let cool for 2 minutes. Then, brush the surfaces with the egg white, and bake for 2 minutes more. Remove from the oven and cool completely. Turn the oven down to 325°F/160°C for the almonds.

To make the pastry cream, in a heavy stainless steel pot combine the half-and-half, 2.3 ounces/65 g sugar, salt and vanilla bean. Bring to a simmer, stirring occasionally to dissolve the sugar. While this is heating, whisk the egg yolks in a large bowl until combined, and whisk in the 0.8 ounces/22 g sugar until it looks smooth and creamy, about 15 seconds. Whisk in the cornstarch until pale yellow, about 30 seconds more.

Once the half-and-half mixture is simmering, set your bowl with the eggs in it on top of a dish towel to create a stabilizing rest for it and slowly add the hot liquid to the bowl of egg yolks, whisking the entire time. Once all of the dairy is added and thoroughly mixed (the mixture will have thickened a bit), return it to the pot and bring it to a boil over medium heat. The boiling will look like a few huge, gloppy bubbles. Mix vigorously the whole time with a whisk or else you will scramble your eggs. It will have thickened even further at this point. Remove the custard from the heat. Cube and soften the butter and whisk with custard until completely melted and combined. Strain through a fine-mesh metal strainer.

Cover the surface of the pastry cream directly with plastic wrap to prevent a skin from forming. Chill until set. Once cold, use immediately, or refrigerate for up to 3 days.

To toast the almonds, spread on a sheet pan and toast in the oven for about 10 minutes, until lightly brown. Let cool.

ASSEMBLING THE TARTLETS

Cover the bottom of the tart shells with a single layer of the toasted almonds, reserving a few to garnish the top of each tart. Cover the almonds with about 2.5 ounces/70 g of the pastry cream per tart. Smooth the tops.

Cut the strawberries in half and lay them on paper towels to absorb any liquid. This way they will be less likely to bleed onto the surface of the pastry cream. Then, place four to seven halves on top of the pastry cream, cut side down with the tips facing in toward the center. Garnish the middle of the tart with a small amount of the toasted almonds. A sprig of mint also adds a pop of color and fragrance. Refrigerate these tarts until serving. They are best assembled the day you want to serve them.

RICOTTA TRIPTYCH I:
HONEYED RICOTTA AND PISTACHIO TARTS

These tarts are quite beautiful. The contrast of the bright white filling,
the green pistachios and the brightly colored edible pansy really catches the eye.
Your belly will also take notice. This tart is lightly sweetened with orange blossom
honey from Maine, but any honey will do. The candied pistachios on top help
to give a special little bonus crunch.

YIELD: Eight 4-in/10-cm tartlets

CRUST

1.25 oz/35 g pistachios, chopped

5 oz/140 g cold unsalted butter

7.75 oz/220 g all-purpose flour

1 oz/30 g granulated sugar

1 tsp/7 g fine sea salt

1.25 oz/35 ml ice water

1 egg white, beaten with a fork

CANDIED PISTACHIOS

1 cup/115 g pistachios

4 tbsp/50 g turbinado sugar

1 oz/30 ml hot water

1 oz/30 g granulated sugar

HONEYED RICOTTA FILLING

14 oz/400 g high-quality, self-draining whole-milk ricotta cheese such as Calabro Ricotta cheese

1.75 oz/50 g orange blossom honey (or your favorite honey)

8 food-grade fresh pansy blossoms (or other small edible flower)

For the crust, preheat the oven to 350°F/180°C. Toast the pistachios for 10 minutes. When cool, finely chop them and set aside. Next, cut your cold butter into ½-inch/1-cm cubes and keep cold until you are ready to mix the dough. Measure out about half of the flour and add the sugar and salt to it, toss to combine and throw in your butter as well. Break the butter in with your fingers by rubbing it between your thumb and fingers. Do this until no lumps are present and a dough has formed. This will take some time and working with your hands.

Add the chopped pistachios to the other half of the flour. Add this mixture to the butter-flour mixture and work it all together with your hands until the flour is mostly incorporated. When the dough has lost most of its dusty appearance, add the ice water and mix until completely combined. Then, press the dough into a circle or rectangle and wrap with plastic wrap. Chill for at least 1 hour. This dough can be wrapped tightly and refrigerated for 3 days or frozen for longer storage.

Roll the dough out to ⅛ inch/3 mm thick and cut eight 5-inch/12-cm circles out of the dough. Set them into fluted tartlet pans and trim the tops so they are flush with the top of the pan. Chill the shells for another 30 minutes, or overnight.

Preheat the oven to 375°F/190°C.

Prick the bottoms of the tart shells with a fork, place all the tart pans on a sheet pan and then fit aluminum foil or parchment paper into the shells and fill completly with dried beans or rice to weight them down. Bake in the middle of the oven for 30 minutes, rotating the sheet pan after 15 minutes. Remove the beans and foil and bake for another 8 to 10 minutes. The shells should be golden brown and completely dried out. Remove them from the oven and cool for 2 minutes. Brush the surfaces with the beaten egg white, and return them to the oven for 2 minutes more. This helps to seal the shells against the wet filling. Cool completely before removing them from their pans and assembling.

For the candied pistachios, combine the pistachios with the turbinado sugar in a bowl. Put the hot water and granulated sugar in a bowl and stir to dissolve the sugar. Next, add this liquid to the nuts. Toss to coat the nuts thoroughly. Pour the entire mixture on a parchment-lined sheet pan and bake at 350°F/180°C for 10 minutes, rotating after 5 minutes. Cool the nuts and break them apart. Use immediately or store in an airtight container for up to 2 weeks.

For the honeyed ricotta filling, put both ingredients in a food processor fitted with the blade attachment and process until the cheese is shiny, there are no lumps and there is no grainy texture. Stop halfway through and fold the cheese once in the food processor in order to blend it evenly. Use immediately, or store in the refrigerator for up to 4 days.

ASSEMBLING THE TARTLETS

Fill the tart shells evenly with the ricotta filling, about 2 ounces/50 g each. Place one flower in the center of the tart and then place five candied pistachios staggered next to one another coming out of the flower. Chill for 1 hour before serving. The tart can be assembled (except for the flowers and pistachios) the night before; simply add the garnishes before serving.

RICOTTA TRIPTYCH II
BLUEBERRY-LEMON CORNMEAL TART

These ingredients are pretty much made for each other. This tart is one of our favorites. It's refreshing and simple to make. In-season blueberries are the best way to go, but strawberries pair quite nicely as well if you can't wait for blueberry season to hit. You will have quite a bit of extra candied lemon zest, but it keeps for 6 months in the refrigerator.

YIELD: One 8-in/20-cm tart

CRUST

4 oz/110 g all-purpose flour

2 oz/60 g corn flour

¼ tsp/2 g fine sea salt

¼ tsp/1 g lemon zest

3 oz/75 g granulated sugar

3.8 oz/107 g unsalted butter, softened

1.25 oz/35 g egg yolk

1 scant tbsp/15 ml cold water

1 egg white, lightly beaten

FILLING

10 oz/300 g high-quality, whole-milk, self-draining ricotta cheese such as Calabro Ricotta cheese

1.5 oz/40 g granulated sugar

1 tsp/4 g lemon zest

¼ tsp/4 ml vanilla extract

CANDIED LEMON ZEST

Zest of 3 lemons

6 oz/170 ml cold water

2 oz/50 g agave nectar

8 oz/250 g granulated sugar

About 56 blueberries

For the crust, mix the flours and salt together. Combine the lemon zest and sugar, rubbing together with your hands in order to release the lemon oils into the sugar. The sugar will become moist and fragrant.

Add the butter to the bowl with the sugar and zest and mix with a rubber spatula or wooden spoon until the ingredients are evenly combined and there are no lumps and a smooth paste has formed. Then, add the egg yolks in three additions. You will need to stir and scrape down to the bottom of the bowl to fully incorporate each addition. Add the dry ingredients, and mix until evenly combined. This mixture will be quite soft.

Add the water and mix to incorporate into the dough; you may need to use your hands to do this. The dough will be soft and a bit sticky. Chill the dough well for at least 1 hour before rolling out. This dough can be wrapped tightly in plastic and refrigerated for at least 3 days or frozen for longer storage.

Preheat the oven to 375°F/190°C.

Roll the dough out to about ⅛ inch/3 mm thick and cut one 10-inch/25-cm circle out of it. Put an 8-inch/20-cm flan ring on a parchment-lined sheet pan, and fit the 10-inch/25-cm circle into it. You will need to trim the top of the tart dough to be flush with the top of the ring. Make sure to gently press the dough all the way into the corners of the ring. Patch as needed.

Chill the dough for at least 30 minutes, prick a few times all over the bottom with a fork and then blind-bake the shell. Take aluminum foil or parchment paper and fit it into the circle. Add dried beans or rice to the aluminum foil all the way up to the top of the ring. Position the rack in the middle of the oven. Bake the shell for 35 minutes, rotating the pan halfway through. Remove the pie weights and parchment or foil and bake for another 10 minutes or until the shell is golden brown and completely dried out. Cool for 2 minutes, then brush the bottom and sides with egg white and return it to the oven for 2 minutes. Cool completely before filling.

To make the ricotta filling, mix all of the filling ingredients in a food processor until completely smooth and shiny. Use immediately, or refrigerate in an airtight container for up to 4 days.

For the candied lemon zest, put the zest in a heavy-bottom stainless steel pot and cover with cold water. Bring the water to a boil, and then drain. Repeat this process twice more using fresh cold water. This helps reduce the bitterness.

Combine the zest with the water, agave nectar and granulated sugar in the pot. Bring to a boil. Reduce the heat to a low simmer and cook for about 20 minutes, until zest is translucent. Watch that the sugar syrup does not caramelize. Cool and store the syrup in the refrigerator for up to 6 months.

ASSEMBLING THE TART

Fill the tart shell up to the edge with the lemon ricotta filling. Next, place the berries in three concentric circles, starting from the outside edge going in toward the center. In the very center, arrange a pile of the candied lemon zest. This tart can be prepared up to 1 day in advance. Keep refrigerated until serving.

RICOTTA TRIPTYCH III
CHOCOLATE-RASPBERRY RICOTTA TARTS

Ricotta cheese is fantastic for both sweet and savory dishes. The quality of the cheese matters a lot, especially when using it in pastries, so we use a beautiful whole-milk ricotta by the name of Calabro, made in Connecticut with milk from Vermont cows. This cheese is packed in a distinctive plastic-covered, self-draining tin, which helps to make sure most of the water has drained off, leaving a thick ricotta that is not at all grainy. It has a wonderfully clean, fresh milk taste and is a great example of how a high-quality ingredient can make all the difference in the end product. When paired with some sugar and fresh vanilla bean, it's closer to vanilla ice cream than to any cheese. We eat it by the spoonful!

YIELD: Eight 4-in/10-cm tartlets

CHOCOLATE SHORT DOUGH

5 oz/140 g flour

2.8 oz/80 g unsweetened cocoa powder

¼ tsp/2 g fine sea salt

5 oz/140 g unsalted butter, softened

6 oz/175 g granulated sugar

¼ tsp/4 ml vanilla extract

0.4 oz/11 g egg yolks

1 egg white, lightly beaten

RASPBERRY JAM

2 quarts/2 L raspberries

⅓ cup/80 ml water

1 tbsp/15 ml lemon juice

1 (1.75 oz/50 g) package pectin, such as Ball Original Fruit Pectin

42 oz/1 kg granulated sugar

VANILLA BEAN RICOTTA FILLING

1 lb/450 g ricotta cheese (high quality, whole milk self-draining, ricotta cheese such as Calabro Ricotta cheese)

3.5 oz/100 g granulated sugar

½ vanilla bean, split and scraped

56 fresh raspberries

1 bar of your favorite chocolate, for making chocolate curls

For the crust, mix the flour, cocoa powder and salt together. Next, combine the butter, sugar and vanilla extract in a bowl. Mix it with a wooden spoon or rubber spatula until it is smooth and there are no lumps and a smooth paste has formed. Add the egg yolks and mix to combine. Add the dry ingredients and mix until all the ingredients are evenly combined to form a very dark, almost black, tart dough. Chill the dough for about 30 minutes before rolling out. This dough can also be chilled overnight, but it will need to be warmed up before rolling it out or it will crack. If it does, however, it is easy to mold back together by pushing it back with your fingertips. It will also freeze well wrapped tightly in plastic wrap.

Roll the dough out to about ⅛ inch/3 mm on a floured surface and cut the circles out with a 4 ½-inch to 5-inch/11 to 12-cm circular cutter. Immediately set these circles into eight ungreased 4-inch/10-cm fluted tartlet pans. Mold the dough to the shape of the pans, trimming the excess dough all around the edge, making it flush with the top. Chill the tart dough for at least 1 hour or up to overnight. After it is chilled, prick it with a fork before baking to decrease the bubbling up of the dough, as well as to ward off shrinkage during the baking process.

Preheat the oven to 375°F/190°C with a rack in the middle. These tart shells do not need to be blind-baked with pie weights. The tart dough stays put during baking. Bake the shells for 16 minutes, rotating the tray of tart shells once after 8 minutes. Remove the shells from the oven and let sit for 2 minutes. Take the egg white and brush it onto the surface of the shells, including the sides, then put it back in the oven for 2 minutes. This helps to seal the surface of the shell to ward off sogginess brought on by the wet filling. Cool completely before use.

For the raspberry jam, combine the raspberries, water, lemon juice and pectin in a sauce pot. Stir and bring to a boil over high heat, stirring as needed to prevent scorching. Add the sugar and stir to dissolve. Bring it all back to a rolling boil that cannot be stirred down. Boil like that for 1 minute. If you fail to boil it this hard, the pectin may not activate fully and the jam will be runny. Skim the scum and store the jam in an airtight container in the refrigerator.

For the vanilla bean ricotta filling, put the cheese, sugar and vanilla bean seeds in a food processor. Process the mixture until smooth and somewhat shiny. Give it a stir and process a little more. No lumps or graininess should be present. Use immediately or store for up to 4 days in the refrigerator.

ASSEMBLING THE TARTLETS

Fill each tart shell with 2 ounces/50 g of the ricotta filling. The filling should come up to the edge of the crust. Place seven raspberries around the outer edge of the filling, or in any way you find pleasing, and use a vegetable peeler to shave chocolate curls, arranging them in the center of each tart. Keep chilled until serving. These can be made up to 1 day in advance. If there is any extra filling and raspberries, feel free to just gobble them up together. You won't be sorry.

SUMMER IN A CRUST: A&J'S CLASSIC ORCHARD PEACH TARTS

There is no pastry item that we look forward to more than this summer tart, which might be the perfect combination of flaky crust and luscious fruit. Crates of peaches, right off the tree, are sourced from Cider Hill Farm in Amesbury, Massachusetts, and we get to pick them up directly at the Marblehead Farmers' Market every Saturday morning while they're in season. If your peaches are fresh and local—or better yet, if you picked them yourself—these tarts are hard to beat after a grilled dinner and sweet corn. They taste like summer.

YIELD: Six 5-in/12-cm tartlets

1 recipe Lazy Baker's Puff Pastry Dough (page 185)

5 medium peaches

8 oz/250 g granulated sugar

2 ½ tsp/8 g cornstarch

Egg wash, consisting of 1 beaten egg and a splash of water

Spray six 5-inch/12-cm flan rings with cooking spray. Roll our your dough to 14 inches × 27 inches/35 × 70 cm, cut out six 7-inch/18-cm circles and place on top of the flan rings. Lifting up around the entire perimeter of the disk, "settle" the dough into the corners of the rings. Then, working from the outside in, roll the overlapping dough until you can press the roll into the side of the flan ring, creating a thicker outer crust with a thin bottom. Place on a sheet pan and chill in the refrigerator until ready to use.

Cut the peaches into wedges, ¾ inch/2 cm wide (skin side) at the most. You should be able to get about 10 slices per peach. In a large bowl, toss the peaches with the sugar and let sit for 30 minutes to macerate.

Preheat the oven to 450°F/230°C, with the baking stone in place.

Add the cornstarch to the macerated peaches and toss again. Egg wash the rims of the crust and arrange the slices in the pastry dough rings as artfully as you wish, fitting roughly eight slices per ring.

Bake on the baking stone for 15 minutes. Raise the pan to the upper shelf and rotate the pan as well. Continue to bake for 20 to 25 additional minutes, rotating as necessary to create a uniformly golden crust. Make sure to check the bottoms by lifting the edge of the tart with a spatula and peeking. Bake until the filling boils and the edges of the peaches begin to brown. Remove the rings immediately after they come out of the oven to avoid sticking to the pastry, and move the tarts to a cooling rack. Give them at least 15 minutes to cool before handling or eating.

PEAR-CARAMEL PIE

This is a wonderfully comforting fall and winter pie. Pears spiced lightly with cinnamon and ginger are made all the richer by brown sugar and homemade caramel. Make the caramel first so that it has time to cool. Any leftover caramel can be used to garnish each slice of pie or save for future use. The caramel will keep for 1 week at room temperature in an airtight container or in the refrigerator for a few weeks.

YIELD: One 9-in/23-cm double-crust deep-dish pie

CRUST

1 recipe 3-2-1 Pie Dough (page 187)

CARAMEL

10.5 oz/300 g granulated sugar

4 oz/110 ml water

9.65 oz/270 ml heavy cream

1.75 oz/50 g unsalted butter, cubed, softened

FILLING

3 lbs/1.5 kg pears, peeled and medium diced

5 oz/140 g brown sugar

2 ½ tsp/6 g ground cinnamon

¼ tsp/0.5 g ground nutmeg

1 tsp/2.5 g ground ginger

½ tsp/3 g fine sea salt

6 tbsp/2 g all-purpose flour

Egg wash, consisting of 1 beaten egg and a splash of water

For the crust, roll the dough into two circles about 12 inches/30 cm in diameter. The bottom piece should be a little bit bigger, to cover the pie dish. Fit the bottom into the dish and chill until you are ready to put the filling in and top it. Chill the top piece as well until you are ready to completely assemble the pie.

For the caramel, combine the sugar and water in a large very clean saucepan over high heat. Make sure all the utensils you use are very clean as impurities can cause your caramel to crystallize. Stir it with a spatula to dissolve the sugar. Have a pastry brush and a cup/240 ml of water ready to wash down the sides of the pot. Bring this mixture to a boil. Once it is boiling, you will want to wash down the sides of the pot periodically to prevent crystallization. It should become a deep amber/caramel, which is about 325˚F/160°C on a candy thermometer.

When the caramel is the right color, slowly whisk the cream into the sugar syrup, being very careful to avoid the steam that will burst up toward your hand. Continue to cook the caramel for 2 minutes. Remove the pot from the heat and stir in the butter.

For the filling, peel and cut the fruit. Combine it with all of the dry ingredients, tossing until evenly coated. Allow the fruit to sit for 30 minutes.

ASSEMBLING THE PIE

Preheat the oven to 450°F/230°C, with the baking stone in place.

Pull the pie dish from the fridge along with the top circle of the pie. Trim the overhanging edge of the bottom crust with a knife. Toss the fruit again, and then pour it all into the pie dish. Pour 1 cup/340 g of caramel evenly over the top of the fruit. Egg wash the rim of the bottom crust lightly, and then put on the top piece. Crimp the edge of the pie to seal it and create a decorative edge by putting the thumb and index finger of your nondominant hand together and pressing the dough into that wedge with your other index finger in order to create a point. Do this all the way around the rim of the pie. Cut six slits in the pie evenly spaced on the top piece, and egg wash the top and the edge. Place directly on the baking stone, and bake for 1 hour. The top needs to be a deep golden brown and the filling should be bubbling. If it is taking too long, raise the pie up on the rack so that it gets more direct heat. It may take another 10 minutes to bubble and color. Remove the pie from the oven and cool for 6 hours or more before serving to allow the filling to set. Serve warm or at room temperature.

Drizzle extra caramel on top when plating each piece. Boom!

MAPLE-WALNUT SWEET POTATO PIE

The maple-walnut topping does two things for the humble sweet potato pie. It gives it added texture and it gives this Southern classic an intriguing, Northeast twist. Maple sugar can be found at most high-end grocery stores or health food stores. This recipe uses our standard 3-2-1 Pie Dough, but with slightly different ingredient weights to yield one bottom crust.

YIELD: One 9-in/23-cm single-crust pie

CRUST

9 oz/250 g all-purpose flour

6 oz/175 g unsalted butter

3 oz/85 ml ice water

¾ tsp/5 g fine sea salt

Egg wash, consisting of 1 beaten egg and a splash of water

FILLING

1 lb 12 oz/800 g sweet potato or yam purée

6 oz/175 g yolks

6 oz/175 g sour cream

1.75 oz/50 ml milk

1.25 oz/35 ml spiced rum or bourbon

6.75 oz/190 g brown sugar

MAPLE WALNUT TOPPING

7 oz/200 g walnut halves and pieces

1 oz/30 g maple sugar

1.5 oz/45 g granulated sugar

Pinch of fine sea salt

1 oz/30 g unsalted butter, melted

For the crust, preheat the oven to 425°F/220°C, with the baking stone in place.

Make the crust according to the instructions on page 187. Roll the dough out to a circle about ⅛ inch/3 mm thick. To test the size, try fitting it into the 9-inch/23-cm pie pan. You should have about 2 inches/5 cm of overhang all the way around. Chill the whole thing for at least 30 minutes. Trim the overhanging edge a bit, but do not trim it completely to the edge of the pie plate. Pinch the extra edge decoratively by putting the thumb and index finger of your nondominant hand together and pressing the dough into that wedge with your other index finger in order to create a point. Continue this along the entire edge of the pie.

Next, insert aluminum foil or parchment into the cavity of the pie dish and fill it to the top with dried beans or rice as weights. Egg wash the crimped edge and bake for 30 minutes directly on the baking stone. Remove the weights and foil or parchment and prick the bottom of the pie with a fork a few times. Rotating the dish, put it back in the oven for another 20 minutes, until the bottom is golden and dried out. If you are worried about the edge getting too dark, cover it with aluminum foil. Cool completely.

For the filling, put the sweet potato purée in a bowl, add the rest of the ingredients and mix until evenly combined. You can refrigerate the filling for up to 1 day before using it.

For the topping, combine the walnuts, sugars and salt in a food processor and pulse until you reduce the walnuts to the size of small peas. Or, chop the walnuts to the same size and combine them with the other dry ingredients. Pour the melted butter over the mixture, and mix it together with your fingers. Store in the refrigerator for up to 1 month in an airtight container.

ASSEMBLING THE PIE

Preheat the oven to 350°F/180°C, and set the rack in the middle of the oven. Before filling the pie shell, make an aluminum foil collar for the edge of the pie shell to protect it from burning.

If the filling has been refrigerated, bring it to room temperature before assembling the pie. Pour all of the filling into the shell and smooth out the top. Then, evenly cover the top of the custard with 7 ounces/200 g of maple topping so that it covers right to the edge of where it meets the shell. Place it in the oven and bake for 70 to 80 minutes, rotating once for even browning. If the topping is getting too dark, cover the top with a piece of foil. Look for the sides to set while the middle of the filling still jiggles a bit when gently shaken. Remove from the oven and cool to room temperature before cutting. This pie can be stored in the fridge for a few days.

NOTE: *Pie Cookie Cut-Outs.* If you have some extra dough scraps from rolling out/trimming your pie shell, decorate the top of this pie with some easy cookie cutouts. Reroll the scrap dough to about ⅛ inch/3 mm thick, and cut with whatever shaped cutters you have on hand; we like the maple leaf to complement the topping. Toss them on a parchment-lined sheet pan, spray with water or brush with beaten egg, sprinkle with cinnamon sugar and bake at 425°F/220°C for 20 minutes, or until golden brown. Arrange them on the top of the pie after it's cooled.

SHE DON'T USE JELLY: CONCORD GRAPE PIE

When we opened the bakery in 2006, we spent 2 years living with Jackie's parents while our big small business gamble got off its feet. Jackie's dad, Tom, has a green thumb that would make leprechauns jealous. Part of his Babylon-esque garden is a twisting vine of Concord grapes, and we wondered out loud at work what we should do with all of the beautiful fruit it was producing. Our first full-time baker and full-time locavore, Sarah, introduced us to this quintessentially New England treat. If you have kids, get them to slip the skins off the grapes. It's easy to do, will get their hands a little sticky (that's a selling point for kids) and you can accept it as prepayment for the best little pies the early fall has to offer.

YIELD: Four 5-in/12-cm mini pies

CRUST

21 oz/600 g very cold all-purpose flour

2 ½ tsp/17 g fine sea salt

14 oz/400 g very cold unsalted butter

7 oz/200 ml ice water

CONCORD GRAPE FILLING

27 oz/765 g stemmed Concord grapes

8.75 oz/250 g granulated sugar

4 tbsp/1.5 g all-purpose flour

Egg wash, consisting of 1 beaten egg and a splash of water

For the crust, follow the procedure on page 187 for mixing and rolling the dough. Roll the dough out to about 18 inches × 22 inches/45 × 55 cm, about ⅛ inch/3 mm thick, and use a 6-inch/15-cm cutter to cut eight circles. Line four 5-inch/12-cm × 1-inch/2.5-cm mini pie pans with circles of dough, pressing it into the sides and corners and trimming any excess off along the edge. The dough edge should go all the way to the edge of the lip of the pan. Chill the lined pans and remaining dough circles until the filling is ready.

For the filling, slip the skins of the grapes off the pulpy interior. Collect the green pulp, seeds and all, into a heavy-bottom pot, and reserve the skins off to the side. Heat the pulp gently over medium heat, and then turn to high heat to achieve a boil. Boil for 3 minutes to soften the pulp, stirring to prevent scorching. Strain the pulp through a wire-mesh sieve, pushing all the pulp through, and discard the seeds. Add the skins to the pulp and stir. Refrigerate for up to 1 day, or move on to the next step.

(If reheating from the refrigerator, reheat the filling to a boil and remove from the heat.) Mix together the sugar and flour and then add it to the hot mixture. Stir to break up clumps. Set aside to cool to around 100°F/40°C before using.

ASSEMBLING THE PIES

Preheat the oven to 450°F/230°C, with the baking stone in place.

Fill the chilled pie bottoms to just below the rim with the warm filling, and egg wash the rim where the top crust will connect to the bottom. Place the top crust on the filled bottom crust, and crimp the edge into decorative points by putting the index finger and thumb of your nondominant hand together and then taking the index finger of your dominant hand and pressing it into that space to create points with the dough. Trim the excess dough off the sides of the pan after crimping. Cut three or four slits in the top of the crust, then move on to the next pie. When all are complete, egg wash the top crusts, place all pies on a sheet pan and place the pan directly on the baking stone. If it takes you awhile to crimp each one, it may be wise to put each one in the fridge while you finish the others just to keep the dough from melting. You can egg wash them before or after refrigerating.

Bake for 25 minutes on the baking stone, rotating after 12 minutes. Move the pies to a higher shelf, and continue baking for 15 to 20 minutes, or until you see the filling bubbling and the crust is a uniform dark golden brown. Let the pies rest 5 minutes in their pans before removing with an offset spatula. Be careful to release any stuck edges before lifting from the pan. Let cool for 1 hour or more before eating. The longer you wait, the more set the filling will become.

THE CLASSIC A&J APPLE TART

The apple tart was one of the first seasonal tarts we had on the menu when we first opened, and it has stayed ever since. It's the first tart Jackie used the Lazy Baker's Puff Pastry Dough recipe for (this version uses ½ of that recipe), and it was immediately evident that the dough and apples were made for each other. It is a customer favorite, and many are sad to see it go when Brooksby Farm in Peabody, Massachusetts, closes down after New Year's and our local apple supply dries up. But there's always next year!

YIELD: One 8-in/20-cm tart

CRUST

5.5 oz/155 g all-purpose flour

½ tsp/1.5 g baking powder

Scant ½ tsp/1.5 g fine sea salt

6.5 oz/180 g butter

3.25 oz/90 g sour cream

FILLING

1 lb/450 g Cortland Apples, peeled and cut into 1"/2.5-cm wedges

4 oz/100 g granulated sugar

¾ tsp/2 g ground cinnamon

2 tbsp/1 g all-purpose flour

CRUMB TOPPING

3.5 oz/70 g all-purpose flour

3.5 oz/100 g granulated sugar

Scant ¼ tsp/2 g fine sea salt

½ tsp/1 g ground cinnamon

3 oz/75 g unsalted butter, melted

½ tsp/2 ml vanilla extract

Egg wash, consisting of 1 beaten egg and a splash of water

For the crust, follow the instructions for the Lazy Baker's Puff Pastry on page 185. Roll your dough to about 6 inches × 10 inches/15 × 25 cm instead of the 6 inches × 16 inches/15 × 40 cm in the full recipe, and then follow the folding instructions as directed. After you have rested and chilled the dough, roll it out to a 14-inch/35-cm square and cut out one 12-inch/30-cm circle. Spray an 8-inch/20-cm flan ring with cooking spray and place on a sheet pan. Lifting up around the entire perimeter of the dough disk, "settle" the dough into the corners of the flan ring. Then, working from the outside in, roll the overlapping dough until you can press the roll into the side of the ring, creating a thicker outer crust with a thin bottom. Chill until ready to use.

For the filling, toss the apples in the dry ingredients and let macerate for 30 minutes. While you're waiting, make the topping.

For the topping, combine all the dry ingredients in a bowl. Pour the butter over the dry ingredients and combine with your fingers until completely moistened. This will keep in the fridge for at least 1 month in an airtight container. Before using, however, make sure it is at room temperature.

ASSEMBLING THE TART

Preheat the oven to 450°F/230°C, with the baking stone in place.

Egg wash the rim of the dough before filling. Pile all of your apple mixture into the tart dough, making sure it is evenly distributed right to the edge; it will seem like a lot. Bake directly on the baking stone for 15 minutes. Remove from the oven, and crumble the topping on top of the apples, breaking it apart with your fingers and layering it evenly over the top. Raise the pan to the upper shelf, rotating it as well. Continue to bake for another 30 to 40 minutes, rotating as necessary to create a uniformly golden crust—make sure to check the bottom as well. Bake until deep golden brown all over. Remove the ring immediately after it comes out of the oven to avoid sticking to the pastry, and move the tart to the cooling rack. Serve warm or at room temperature. A scoop of vanilla ice cream certainly wouldn't hurt, but this tart on its own packs a rich, buttery punch, so be forewarned!

SPIKED PECAN PIE

Jackie came up with this version of a pecan pie just before Thanksgiving one year. She is partial to pecan pies that are not ridiculously sweet and that have a soft, almost custard-like texture to the filling. We got pretty liberal with the bourbon here, which gives the pie some heat and also helps to temper the sweetness. This uses the 3-2-1 Pie Dough, but in different ingredient amounts.

YIELD: One 9-in/23-cm single-crust pie

CRUST

9 oz/250 g all-purpose flour

¾ tsp/5 g fine sea salt

6 oz/175 g unsalted butter

3 oz/85 ml ice water

FILLING

15 oz/425 g brown sugar

15 oz/425 g agave nectar or corn syrup

4 oz/100 g unsalted butter

¾ tsp/5 g fine sea salt

10 oz/280 eggs

3.25 oz/90 ml heavy cream

2.5 oz/70 ml bourbon

1 tbsp/15 ml vanilla extract

6 oz/175 g pecan halves

Egg wash, consisting of 1 beaten egg and a splash of water

For the filling, heat the brown sugar, agave, butter and salt in a heavy-bottom medium stainless steel pot. Bring it just to a boil and then remove from the heat. Cool this mixture down to 100°F–120°F/38°C–50°C. You can hasten the process by putting it in the fridge. If it gets too cool, though, it may solidify. You would then want to gently warm it to melt it before adding the rest of the ingredients.

Beat the eggs, cream, bourbon and vanilla in a bowl and add it all to the sugar mixture. Whisk it together until you have a smooth mixture.

ASSEMBLING THE PIE

Preheat the oven to 450°F/230°C, with the baking stone in place.

Remove the chilled crust from the refrigerator and line the bottom of the crust with the pecan halves flat side down in a single layer. If they do not all fit, just hold them aside until after you have poured in the filling. Pour the filling into the crust and note that the pecans are floating to the top. Add the rest of the pecans to the surface of the custard until the surface is completely filled with nuts. Finally, egg wash the edge of the pie dough.

Carefully put your pie in the oven, directly on the baking stone, and immediately turn the oven down to 425°F/220°C. Bake for 50 to 60 minutes. The filling should be a little jiggly in the very center, but mostly set, with a spongy, firm feeling to the top. If the edge of the crust is getting too dark, cover it with aluminum foil. Cool completely and serve at room temperature.

SALTED CARAMEL-CASHEW TART

Most of our recipes are derived from our putting our heads together with staff members. One of our pastry bakers, Mariel, helped me come up with this one just before she went on maternity leave. We needed an early fall dessert when the fruits were all disappearing, and Mariel brought this one to life. Cashews, cardamom and caramel combine to make a slightly exotic combination. The Spiced Caramel makes about twice as much as you need for one tart. Store leftovers at room temperature in an airtight container for 1 week or in the refrigerator for a few weeks.

YIELD: One 8-in/20-cm tart

CARDAMOM PÂTE SUCRÉE

8 oz/230 g all-purpose flour

2 oz/50 g granulated sugar

3 pinches fine sea salt

Scant ½ tsp/1 g finely ground cardamom seeds

5 oz/140 g cold unsalted butter

1 oz/30 ml heavy cream

0.75 oz/20 g egg yolks

SALTED CASHEWS

½ cup/120 ml water

2 tsp/14 g fine sea salt

3 oz/75 g raw cashews (halves and wholes)

SPICED CARAMEL

7.25 oz/210 ml heavy cream

⅓ vanilla bean, split lengthwise

1 tsp/3 g finely ground cardamom seed

7.85 oz/225 g granulated sugar

3 oz/90 ml water

1.5 oz/45 g unsalted butter, softened

1 tsp/5 g fine sea salt

1 tbsp/10 g sesame seeds

For the crust, mix all of the dry ingredients together in a bowl. Cube your cold butter into ½-inch/1-cm chunks. Rub the butter into the flour-sugar mixture with your hands until a coarse cornmeal-type texture is created. There should be no lumps of butter, but the mixture should not have turned to a paste.

Combine the heavy cream and egg yolks and mix together briefly to combine with a fork or whisk. Then add the egg mixture to your dry mixture and combine it with your hands until an evenly mixed dough forms.

Chill the dough for at least 30 minutes before rolling out. Pâte sucrée can also be chilled overnight but will need to be warmed up before rolling out or it will crack. This dough can be left in the refrigerator for at least 3 days, well wrapped. It will also freeze well.

Roll the chilled dough out to ⅛ inch/3 mm thick and cut a 10-inch/25-cm circle out of the dough. Immediately fit this into an 8-inch/20-cm flan ring set on a parchment-lined sheet pan. Trim the excess to be flush with the edge of the ring. Chill the shell for at least 30 minutes or up to overnight.

Preheat the oven to 375°F/190°C.

After chilling the shell, prick the bottom with a fork. Blind-bake the shell by placing aluminum foil or parchment into the cavity of the tart shell and filling it to the edge with dried beans or rice. Bake for 30 minutes, and then remove the weights and foil or parchment and bake for another 10 to 15 minutes, until the shell is golden brown and completely dried out. Cool the shell completely before assembling the tart.

For the salted cashews, mix the water and salt together until the salt is dissolved. Put the nuts in a bowl and toss with the water mixture. Drain the nuts and toast at 325°F/190°C for 10 to 12 minutes, until they develop a golden hue. Cool completely.

For the spiced caramel, combine the cream, vanilla bean and cardamom in a small saucepan and bring just barely to a simmer. Remove from heat and set aside to steep.

Combine the sugar and water in a large, clean saucepan over high heat. Making sure everything you are using to make the caramel is clean will help to ensure your sugar does not crystallize. Stir with a spatula to dissolve the sugar and bring this mixture to a boil. Once it is boiling, you will want to periodically wash down the sides of the pot with a pastry brush dipped in water to prevent crystallization. It should develop an amber/caramel color.

Remove the vanilla beans from the cream when the caramel is almost at the right color. Slowly whisk the cream into the molten sugar, being careful you do not burn your hand on the steam that will erupt from the pot. Be sure to scrape down the pot the cream was in to get all the vanilla and cardamom that has settled to the bottom. You don't want to leave that all behind! Continue to cook the caramel for no more than 1 minute, then remove the pot from the heat and stir in the butter and salt. Cool completely before using.

ASSEMBLING THE TART

Place the cooled nuts in the cooled shell in a single layer. Pour about 6.5 ounces/180 g of the caramel over the nuts. It should come almost up to the top.

Preheat the oven to 350°F/180°C.

Bake the tart for 15 to 20 minutes. You will know it is done when the caramel bubbles uniformly. Do not stop baking until you see it bubble, or the caramel will be too runny when cooled. Cool completely. Serve at room temperature, or refrigerate if you want it set even firmer. Once it is cool, garnish with the sesame seeds along the outside edge of each tart in about a ½-inch/1-cm band. This tart can be made up to 2 days ahead and stored in the refrigerator.

CHOCOLATE-COCONUT-MACADAMIA TART

This tart is a great cold weather treat. Packed with chocolate and nuts and bound together with a simple, syrupy custard and coconut, it takes on a bit of a candy bar–like taste and texture. The chocolate short dough adds a great chocolaty crunch.

YIELD: One 9-in/23-cm tart

CHOCOLATE SHORT DOUGH

6.25 oz/175 g all-purpose flour

3.5 oz/100 g unsweetened cocoa powder

1 ¼ tsp/9 g fine sea salt

6.5 oz/180 g unsalted butter, softened

7.5 oz/215 g granulated sugar

¼ tsp/4 ml vanilla extract

0.5 oz/15 g egg yolks

FILLING

4.25 oz/120 g macadamia nuts

4.5 oz/130 g eggs

3 oz/75 g granulated sugar

4 oz/100 g brown sugar

¼ tsp/4 ml vanilla extract

¼ tsp/2 g fine sea salt

1.5 oz/45 g unsalted butter, melted

2.5 oz/65 g shredded sweetened coconut

1.5 oz/45 g semisweet or bitter-sweet chocolate chips

½ cup/90 g chopped chocolate, melted just prior to garnishing

For the crust, combine the flour, cocoa powder and salt into a bowl. Next, combine the butter, sugar and vanilla extract into a large bowl with the sugar. Mix it with a wooden spoon or rubber spatula until it is smooth and there are no lumps and a smooth paste has formed. Add the egg yolks and mix to combine. Add the dry ingredients and mix until all the ingredients are evenly combined to form a very dark, almost black, tart dough. Chill the dough for at least 30 minutes before rolling out. This dough can also be chilled overnight, but will need to be warmed up before rolling it out or it will crack. If it does, however, it is easy to mold it back together by pushing it back with your fingertips. The chocolate short dough can be refrigerated for at least 3 days. It will also freeze well when wrapped tightly in plastic wrap.

Roll the dough out to about ⅛ inch/3 mm thick on a floured surface and cut a 10-inch/25-cm circle. Immediately fit the circle into an ungreased 9-inch/23-cm metal pie pan; if you spray the pie pan, the dough will slip down the sides of the pan when baking. Repair any cracks if necessary with extra dough and your fingertips. If you leave the holes the very sticky filling will leak and cause your tart to stick to the pan. The edge of the dough should be flush with the inside edge of the pie pan lip and should not extend out onto the lip. Trim as needed. After fitting the shell into the pan, refrigerate for at least 30 minutes or even overnight. Once the dough is chilled, prick the bottom with a fork to limit the bottom of the shell from bubbling up, as well as to cut down on shrinking.

Preheat the oven to 375°F/190°C.

You do not need to blind-bake this shell with pie weights; the crust stays put! Bake for 12 minutes, rotate the pan and bake for about another 8 minutes. The smell of the chocolate crust will become fragrant and the crust should be dry. Cool completely before filling.

For the filling, toast the macadamia nuts for 8 minutes at 325°F/160°C, but be careful: These nuts burn easily. You want a lightly golden toasted hue, but nothing darker. Whisk the eggs, sugars, vanilla and salt together in a bowl until well combined. Add the melted butter, and stir until an even mixture is reached. Add the nuts, coconut and chocolate chips and stir to incorporate. Use immediately, or make in advance and store in the refrigerator for up to 4 days.

ASSEMBLING THE TART

Pour all of the filling into the cooled tart shell. Bake at 350°F/180°C for 24 minutes. Rotate the pan, cover with aluminum foil and bake for another 10 minutes. The tart is done when the color has reached a golden brown and the middle of the tart puffs up a little. The top of the filling will feel firm.

Cool completely, and then chill for at least a couple of hours before removing it from the pan. To garnish, you can pipe melted chocolate into whatever design you like or you can simply drizzle melted chocolate back and forth over the surface with a fork. This tart can be served cold or at room temperature and keeps in the refrigerator for 1 week.

LEMON CURD MACAROON TART

This tart is a great cold weather/early spring tart, as the bright lemon flavor helps to wake up the palate during a winter of heavy, rich foods. The coconut adds a bit of a tropical feel and was adapted from our macaroon cookie recipe to be nut-free and work as a chewy filling between curd and crust.

YIELD: One 8-in/20-cm tart

CRUST

8 oz/230 g all-purpose flour

2 oz/50 g granulated sugar

3 pinches fine sea salt

5 oz/140 g cold unsalted butter

1 oz/30 ml heavy cream

0.75 oz/20 g egg yolks

LEMON FILLING

1.5 tsp/5 g lemon zest

7.5 oz/215 g granulated sugar

3.25 oz/90 g egg yolks

4 oz/110 ml lemon juice

2.5 oz/65 g unsalted butter

Pinch of fine sea salt

COCONUT FILLING

1.25 oz/35 g egg whites

2 oz/50 g granulated sugar

Pinch of fine sea salt

1 tsp/0.5 g all-purpose flour

¼ tsp/4 ml vanilla extract

½ tsp/2 ml coconut extract

0.35 oz/10 g cream of coconut

2.25 oz/60 g shredded sweetened coconut, plus ⅓ cup/100 g, for garnish

For the crust, combine all of the dry ingredients together in a bowl, then cube your cold butter into ½-inch/1-cm chunks. Rub the butter into the flour-sugar mixture with your hands until you reach a coarse, cornmeal-type texture. There should be no lumps of butter, but the mixture should not have turned to a paste.

Next, combine the heavy cream and the yolks and mix together briefly with a fork or whisk. Add the egg mixture to your dry mixture, and combine it with your hands until an evenly mixed dough forms.

Chill the dough for at least 30 minutes before rolling out. It can also be chilled overnight but will need to be warmed up before rolling out or it will crack. This dough can be stored in the refrigerator for up to 3 days, well wrapped. It will also freeze well.

Roll the chilled dough out to ⅛ inch/3 mm thick and cut a 10-inch/25-cm circle out of the dough. Immediately fit this into an 8-inch/20-cm flan ring on a sheet pan. Trim the excess to be flush with the edge of the ring. Chill the shell for at least 30 minutes or even overnight. After chilling, prick the bottom of the shell with a fork to prevent crust bubbles.

Preheat the oven to 375°F/190°C.

Blind-bake the shell by placing aluminum foil or parchment into the cavity of the tart shell and filling it to the edge with dried beans or rice. Bake for 30 minutes, remove the weights and foil or parchment paper and bake for another 10 to 15 minutes, until the shell is golden brown and completely dried out. Cool the shell completely before assembling the tart.

For the lemon filling, rub the zest and sugar together in a 1-quart/1-L heavy-bottom stainless steel pot until fragrant and moist. Add the egg yolks to the sugar-zest mixture and whisk until combined. Add lemon juice, butter and salt.

Cook on medium-low heat, stirring constantly with a rubber spatula and taking care to drag the spatula along the bottom to avoid scorching or scrambling your eggs. Cook until the butter is melted and the mixture is warmed. Never stop stirring. If you have to stop stirring for some reason, remove the pot from the stove.

Once the mixture is melted and combined, your goal is to see steam rising from the surface, but never boil or even simmer the mixture. If you boil, you'll coagulate the eggs and have scrambled the lemon curd. Stirring constantly with a rubber spatula, cook until the curd coats the back of a spoon and leaves a trace when you run your finger along the spoon's covered surface, about 10 minutes. If you want to use a thermometer, it will thicken around 175°F/80°C.

Strain the curd into a bowl and cover the surface immediately with plastic wrap to prevent the curd from forming a skin. Refrigerate it immediately. After cooling completely, remove the plastic wrap and store in a covered container. The curd should have stiffened at this point. Keep refrigerated until you are ready to fill the tart.

For the coconut filling, whisk the first seven ingredients in a bowl to combine, and then fold in the 2.25 ounces/60 g coconut. Store in the refrigerator. The filling can be made up to 3 days in advance. Keep cold until ready to fill the tart.

ASSEMBLING THE TART:

Preheat the oven to 350°F/180°C.

Toast the ⅓ cup/100 g coconut for about 8 minutes, or until the coconut starts to take on a toasty brown color but with still some white parts showing. Cool.

Fill the cooled shell with all of the coconut filling, spreading it along the bottom. Bake for 10 minutes, until the tips of the coconut start to turn toasty brown. Cool completely. Spread about 14 ounces/400 g of the chilled curd in the tart shell, right to the edge. Garnish with a 1-inch/2.5-cm band of toasted coconut around the outer edge of the tart. Serve immediately, or keep chilled until ready to serve. This tart can be fully prepared up to 2 days in advance.

CHOCOLATE-CINNAMON TARTS

While we often look to source produce and dairy locally, we are also able to source some of our chocolate from the area. Taza Chocolate in Somerville, Massachusetts, is a unique chocolatier. They produce an authentic stone-ground organic chocolate from bean to bar. In this tart, we use their 80 percent dark chocolate along with their chocolate-covered cocoa nibs for garnishing. Nibs are roasted cocoa beans, which in this case are freshly roasted and then covered in chocolate—highly addictive. To highlight the chocolate, we keep this tart simple. Fresh cream, eggs and sugar create a soft, rich chocolate custard lightly spiced with cinnamon, which keeps it from being too one-dimensional. If you can't get your hands on Taza, use any high-quality dark chocolate.

YIELD: Eight 5-in/12-cm tartlets

CHOCOLATE SHORT DOUGH

6.2 oz/175 g all-purpose flour

3.5 oz/100 g unsweetened cocoa powder

¼ tsp/2 g fine sea salt

6.4 oz/180 g unsalted butter, softened

7.5 oz/215 g granulated sugar

¼ tsp/4 ml vanilla extract

0.5 oz/15 g egg yolks

CHOCOLATE CUSTARD

5.5 oz/155 g dark chocolate (preferably 80%)

1 lb 2 oz/510 ml heavy cream

1 ¼ tsp/3 g ground cinnamon

3.7 oz/104 g egg yolks

1.5 oz/45 g granulated sugar

1 tsp/5 ml vanilla extract

1 tbsp/10 g chocolate-covered cocoa nibs, for garnish (optional)

For the crust, combine the flour, cocoa powder and sea salt. Combine the butter, sugar and vanilla extract in a bowl. Mix it with a wooden spoon or rubber spatula until it is smooth and there are no lumps and a smooth paste has formed. Add the egg yolks and mix to combine. Add the dry ingredients and mix until all the ingredients are evenly combined to form a quite dark, almost black, tart dough. Chill the dough for about 30 minutes before rolling out. This dough can also be chilled overnight, but will need to be warmed up before rolling it out or else it will crack. Rolling this dough out a little on the warm side so that it is pliable helps keep it from cracking. However, if it does, it is easy to mold it back together by pushing it back with your fingertips. The chocolate short dough can be refrigerated for at least 3 days. It will also freeze well when wrapped tightly in plastic wrap.

Roll the dough out to a little thicker than ⅛ inch/3 mm thick on a floured surface and cut the circles out with a 5-inch/12-cm diameter cutter. Immediately fit these circles into ungreased mini pie pans; if you spray the molds, the dough will slip down the sides of the pans when baking. Repair any cracks if necessary with extra dough and your fingertips. The edge of the dough should be flush with the inside edge of the pie pan lip and should not extend out onto the lip. Trim as needed. After fitting all the shells into the pans, refrigerate for at least 30 minutes or even overnight. Once the dough is chilled, prick the bottom of each shell with a fork to limit the bottom of the shell from bubbling up, as well as to cut down on shrinking.

Preheat the oven to 375°F/190°C.

You do not need to blind-bake these shells with pie weights; the crust stays put! Bake for 12 minutes, rotate the pans and bake for about another 6 minutes. The smell of the chocolate crust will become fragrant and the crust should be dry. Cool completely before filling. Lower the oven temperature to 350°F/180°C.

For the chocolate filling, place the chocolate in a heatproof bowl. Pour the heavy cream into a heavy-bottom stainless steel pot and add the cinnamon. Whisk the cinnamon and cream together and heat until simmering. Do not boil. Pour this cream over the chocolate and stir until the chocolate is completely melted. Put your yolks into a large bowl. Add the sugar and vanilla to the yolks and whisk. Temper ½ cup/120 ml of the hot chocolate mixture into the egg yolks, whisking the whole time in order to not cook the egg yolks. When it is combined, add the remainder of the hot chocolate mixture into the eggs, making sure to whisk the entire time. If anyone else is around, ask them to hold the bowl while you pour and whisk; otherwise, rest the bowl on a crumpled damp towel to prevent it from spinning. Then, strain this whole mixture through a fine-mesh sieve in order to remove any egg that may be solidified.

ASSEMBLING THE TART:

After straining, immediately fill the shells almost to the top. Do this close to the oven so that you will not have to walk far with a full tray of liquid tarts. Bake the tarts for 12 minutes. The middle of the custard should still be a little jiggly when you take them out.

Cool the tarts for about 10 minutes and then add a garnish of chocolate-covered nibs in the center of the tart, if you wish. Doing this soon after baking allows the nibs to slightly melt and adhere to the surface. Refrigerate for 2 hours or overnight before attempting to remove them from their pans. Serve cold or at room temperature.

DON'T THROW OUT THE SCRAPS!

When you have scrap pastry dough left over after putting together your pies or tarts, you should always make cookies. Every pie-baking grandmother knows this trick. It's not rocket science, just good common sense, and an easy and fun way to use up the extra dough—not to mention a way to get two treats out of one!

THIS TECHNIQUE WORKS WITH PRETTY MUCH ANY OF THE PASTRY DOUGHS IN THIS BOOK:

Gather up the remaining dough and chill if it is too warm and is melting and making your hands sticky. After chilling, roll the dough out about ⅛ inch/3 mm thick and cut into whatever shape you want. The pieces of 3-2-1 Pie Dough and the Lazy Baker's Puff Pastry will puff up quite a bit during the baking process.

Before baking, spray with water or brush with egg wash and sprinkle with cinnamon and sugar. The chocolate short dough needs no embellishment other than a cold glass of whole milk!

Bake at 400°F/200°C for about 20 minutes or until golden brown. Bake the chocolate short dough at 375°F/190°C for about 15 minutes. Different doughs will bake for different times, so keep an eye on your cookies—and don't be afraid to do a taste test to determine whether they're done!

SAVORY TARTS

All five of these savory tarts use the same pastry dough for their crusts: the Lazy Baker's Puff Pastry Dough on page 185. Some of them are set into 5-inch/12-cm flan rings, and some are simply laid flat and topped with various vegetables and cheese. All of these tarts would make a great first course or a simple dinner paired with a salad or soup. The pastry dough is a great template for both sweet and savory foods, so feel free to use the recipes as a jumping-off point for your own ingredient combinations in the future.

OYSTER MUSHROOM, THYME AND CHÈVRE TARTS

We have a real weakness for fresh goat cheese, and we're lucky enough to be surrounded by local producers here in northern Massachusetts. Pairing it with mushrooms and thyme gives you a really traditional, tantalizing, savory treat. The oyster mushrooms add a pretty touch to the presentation, but piled shiitakes (or even raw cultivated enokis) would work just as well.

YIELD: Six 5-in/12-cm tarts

1 recipe Lazy Baker's Puff Pastry Dough (page 185)

1 lb/450 g oyster mushroom stems (reserve the flowery caps for garnish)

3 minced shallots

3 oz/75 g unsalted butter

Fine sea salt

3 oz/80 ml heavy cream

15 sprigs fresh thyme

Egg wash, consisting of 1 beaten egg and a splash of water

6 oz/175 g fresh chèvre, crumbled

Extra-virgin olive oil

Preheat the oven to 450°F/230°C, with the baking stone in place.

For the crust, roll out the dough to about 14 inches × 27 inches/35 × 70 cm, about ⅛ inch/3 mm thick, and cut out six 7-inch/18-cm circles. Place six 5-inch/12-cm flan rings on a parchment-lined sheet pan, and spray with cooking spray. Place one circle on top of each ring. Lifting up around the entire perimeter of the disk, "settle" the dough into the corners of the rings. Then, working from the outside in, roll the overlapping dough until you can press the roll into the side of the flan ring, creating a thicker outer crust with a thin bottom. Chill until ready to use.

Separate the stems from the tops of the oyster mushrooms. Finely chop the stems. Mince the shallots and then sweat them in the butter over medium heat. Once the shallots are soft and translucent, add the chopped mushroom stems to the pan. Cook, stirring occasionally, until the mushrooms brown a bit and all the liquid has evaporated. Season to taste with salt. Turn off the heat and stir in the cream. Coarsely chop 12 sprigs of the thyme and add to the mixture. Set aside to cool.

Once the mixture is cool, assemble the tarts. Egg wash the rim of the pastry crust and put about 2 ounces/50 g of the duxelles in the bottom of the chilled pastry circles, spreading it evenly. Then add 1 ounce/30 g crumbled chèvre in the very center, leaving a ½-inch/1-cm border of the duxelles visible. Toss the tops of the oyster mushrooms lightly in olive oil and sprinkle with a little salt. Place these in the center of the tart on top of the goat cheese.

Bake the tarts directly on the baking stone. After about 10 minutes, the pastry dough will start to puff and may need to be pricked with the tip of a knife or a wooden skewer to release the steam. Otherwise, the tart will keep expanding and blow up; you may need to prick it a few times at various points. Rotate the pan and bake for another 10 minutes. Then, move the pan up to the middle rack and bake for another 20 minutes, until the crust is golden brown and the mushrooms have browned and cooked down a bit. Remove from the oven and remove the rings. Strip the remaining three thyme sprigs of their leaves and sprinkle evenly over the tops of the tarts. Cool and eat warm or at room temperature.

ROASTED PEPPER, OLIVE AND FETA TARTS

This tart has quite a few strongly flavored components, but they have a long history of going well together. The roasted garlic is less potent than you would think, and it really adds richness to the crust. The olives add a punch of bitter, sour and salt, and the feta marries well with them. House-roasted peppers are mild and help to balance the strong flavors of the olives and cheese. Make them yourself, because the jarred ones just can't compare.

YIELD: Six 7-in/18-cm tarts

1 recipe Lazy Baker's Puff Pastry Dough (page 185)

2 heads garlic

Extra-virgin olive oil

3 Roasted Red Peppers (page 138)

3 oz/75 g pitted kalamata olives, coarsely chopped

3 oz/75 g Sicilian olives, coarsely chopped

6 oz/175 g feta cheese (goat cheese also pairs well)

Fresh basil or oregano leaves, for garnish

Preheat the oven to 450°F/230°C, with the baking stone in place.

For the crust, roll out the dough to about 14 x 27 inches/ 35 x 68 cm, about ⅛ inch/3 mm thick, and cut out six 7-inch/18-cm circles. Chill your circles of dough on a parchment-lined sheet pan for at least 30 minutes.

To roast the garlic, cut the top off each bulb and place on enough aluminum foil to wrap it up. Pour about 2 tablespoons/30 ml olive oil on top of each bulb so it seeps inside the cloves and wrap the bulb up in the aluminum foil. Roast for about 30 minutes, and check to see if the cloves are soft. If not, keep cooking until the cloves are very soft. Remove from the oven and cool.

Take your chilled circles of dough from the fridge. Remove the cloves of garlic from the bulb (a good squeeze onto a plate will do it) and smear a thin, even layer onto each circle. Then put about 2.5 ounces/65 g of roasted peppers on each circle, 1 ounce/30 g of olives and 1 ounce/30 g of cheese. Spread these all out evenly.

Bake the pan of tarts directly on the baking stone for 15 minutes. Move the pan to the middle rack and bake for about another 10 minutes, until the tarts are a deep golden brown. Remove from the oven and cool, then chop the basil or oregano leaves and sprinkle over the top of the tart. These tarts can be eaten warm or at room temperature. If you are making these ahead, do not put the herbs on until they are cool or the herbs will turn black.

PANCETTA AND ASPARAGUS TARTS

These are so simple and tasty. When asparagus season rolls around in the spring, you have to give this recipe a try! Andy makes his own pancetta at home, so we always have a chunk of it ready to go. If you're not into home curing, it is readily available at the grocery store as well.

YIELD: Six 5-in/12-cm tarts

1 recipe Lazy Baker's Puff Pastry Dough (page 185)

42 thin spears asparagus, trimmed of woody bottoms

Extra-virgin olive oil

Fine sea salt

3 oz/75 g pancetta, diced small

Egg wash, consisting of 1 beaten egg and a splash of water

Preheat the oven to 450°F/230°C, with the baking stone in place.

For the crust, roll out the dough to about 14 inches × 27 inches/35 × 70 cm, about ⅛ inch/3 mm thick, and cut out six 7-inch/18-cm circles. Place six 5-inch/12-cm flan rings on a parchment-lined sheet pan, and spray with cooking spray. Lay one circle on top of each ring. Lifting up around the entire perimeter of the disk, "settle" the dough into the corners of the rings. Then, working from the outside in, roll the overlapping dough until you can press the roll into the side of the flan ring, creating a thicker outer crust with a thin bottom. Chill until ready to use. Chop off the top 3 inches/7 cm of the asparagus. Hold them off to the side, and dice up the remainder of the spears for a total of 8 ounces/250 g. Toss the diced asparagus with a little bit of olive oil to lightly coat and sprinkle with just a little bit of salt; remember, the pancetta is salty on its own. Add the chopped pancetta to the asparagus and evenly combine it. Egg wash the rim of each crust and fill each tart with 1.5 ounces/45 g of this mixture. Next, lightly toss the asparagus tips with oil, and fan six or seven of them out on top of each of the filled tart shells.

Bake the pan of tarts directly on the baking stone. After about 10 minutes, the pastry dough will start to puff and may need to be pricked with the tip of a knife or a wooden skewer to release the steam. You may need to prick it a few times at various points. Rotate the pan and bake for another 10 minutes. Then, move the pan up to the middle rack and bake for another 20 minutes, until the crust is golden brown and the asparagus has started to shrink slightly and take on a little bit of color. Remove from the oven and remove the rings. Cool and eat warm or at room temperature.

PROSCIUTTO, TARRAGON CREAM AND ONION TARTS

Jackie loves this tart because it is sweet and savory at the same time. We have a leg of prosciutto curing in the basement from when we raised pigs a while back, but we have not had a chance to try it. Putting it in these tarts will be a must when it is ready!

YIELD: Six 5-in/12-cm tarts

1 recipe Lazy Baker's Puff Pastry Dough (page 185)

3 medium onions, sliced ⅛-inch/3-mm thick with core intact to keep each slice together

Extra-virgin olive oil

Fine sea salt

Six 6" × 3"/15 × 7-cm strips of prosciutto

1 egg, beaten with a fork and a splash of water added, for egg wash

1 tbsp/15 g fresh tarragon leaves, plus more for garnish

6 tbsp/90 ml heavy cream

2 tbsp/25 g grated pecorino cheese

Preheat the oven to 425˚F/220°C, with the baking stone in place.

Roll out the dough to about 14 inches × 27 inches/35 × 70 cm, about ⅛ inch/3 mm thick, and cut out six 7-inch/18-cm circles. Place six 5-inch/12-cm flan rings on a parchment-lined sheet pan, and spray with cooking spray. Lay one circle on top of each ring. Lifting up around the entire perimeter of the disk, "settle" the dough into the corners of the rings. Then, working from the outside in, roll the overlapping dough until you can press the roll into the side of the flan ring, creating a thicker outer crust with a thin bottom. Chill until ready to use.

Lay each cut onion out on a parchment-lined sheet pan and sprinkle with olive oil and salt. You will probably need two sheet pans. Roast until soft and starting to color, about 20 minutes. Remove from the oven and cool. Turn the oven temperature up to 450°F/230°C.

Sauté the prosciutto until it starts to shrivel and brown a little bit. Cool and set aside. Egg wash the rim of each tart shell, and place each piece of cooled prosciutto inside the pastry dough. The strip of prosciutto should just fit; your goal is to cover the entirety of the bottom of the tart, so trimming parts of the meat that are too long in order to cover areas of the pastry shell will be necessary. Next, sprinkle about ½ tsp/.5 g of tarragon on the bottom of each tart, on top of the prosciutto. Then add six or so roasted onion slices to each tart, maintaining the fanned-out shape of the onions and filling to the top of the tart shell. Finally, pour 1 tablespoon/15 ml of cream into each tart.

Bake directly on the baking stone for 15 minutes, making sure to pop the pastry bubbles and watching that the liquid doesn't boil over. Move the tarts to the middle rack and bake for another 15 minutes, until the onions start to color and the crust is a deep golden brown. Remove from the oven and remove the rings from the shells. Sprinkle 1 teaspoon/4 g pecorino on top of each tart. Cool, and serve warm or at room temperature. Garnish with three or four tarragon leaves set in the middle of the tart in a fan shape or simply sprinkle over the top. If you add the herbs when the tart is hot, they will wilt and turn army green. For the prettiest presentation, wait until the tarts are cool to add the fresh herb.

TOMATO-BASIL TARTS

Beautifully simple: Ripe in-season tomatoes along with basil and a drizzle of olive oil is a classic combination. But instead of putting it on bread, it's laid out on our flaky, buttery tart dough.

YIELD: Six 7-in/18-cm tarts

1 recipe Lazy Baker's Puff Pastry Dough (page 185)

5 or 6 medium tomatoes

Extra-virgin olive oil

Fine sea salt

18 fresh basil leaves

Preheat the oven to 450°F/230°C, with the baking stone in place.

For the crust, roll out the dough to about 14 inches × 27 inches/35 × 70 cm, about ⅛ inch/3 mm thick, and cut out six 7-inch/18-cm circles. Chill your circles of dough on a parchment-lined sheet pan for at least 30 minutes. In the meantime, slice the tomatoes about ¼ inch/5 mm thick so that you have three or four round slices of tomato to place on each tart.

Lightly brush the surface of the dough all over with olive oil, and place the tomato slices evenly spaced around the circle of dough. Drizzle a little more olive oil, and sprinkle with salt.

Bake directly on the baking stone for 15 minutes. Raise the pan up to the middle rack and bake for another 10 minutes or so, until the tarts are golden brown all over.

Remove from the oven and cool. Garnish with basil leaves and serve while warm or at room temperature. If you are making them ahead, do not put the basil on the tarts until they are completely cool or the basil will turn black.

ACKNOWLEDGMENTS

To our parents: It cannot be stated enough how integral our parents have been to the success of the bakery. Their collective investment in our business and children when A&J King was nothing more than an idea is something we will be eternally grateful for. To Tom and Rita, who let us completely take over their lives (and home) for two years: We are all so lucky to have your amazing support day in and day out. To Peter and Joanne, for making so many trips up from Providence to be with the kids, as well as your amazing generosity and advice.

To our family: Big Nonno, Nana 'Nita, Great-Great Grandma, Grandma and Papa, Toby and Casey, Eric and Caroline, Michelle and Dave, Greg and Nichole, Charlie, Russell, Henry, Grace and Gherig. Also thanks to the DiGregorios (especially Uncle Joe); the Develis; and the power trio of Brian, Natalie and Desmond.

To all the folks who have worked for us, put in hours to grow the bakery or helped us develop as bakers and bakery owners: All of our bakers, past and present, retail staff and drivers for putting up with our insanity and giving us the best of yourselves. Non-staff bonus points to Eric Laurits (Eric Laurits Photography), Emily Laurits (we almost ruined your wedding—we're sorry!), Russ Tanzer, Nina Simonds, Jim Jordan (Century Bank), Chris Joachim (Northeast Service Technicians), Alan Spear (Coffee By Design), Matt James, Alison Pray, Tim Gosnell, Dave Tozeski, Sara Deane and the amazing crew at the Standard Baking Co. in Portland, Maine. First dibs shout out goes to William Kiester, who approached two bakers and helped turn them into authors, and his crack design and editorial staff at Page Street Publishing, for putting up with food service countenance in an office environment. Last, but not least, to our regulars in Salem, Massachusetts, who keep our bakery afloat. Without you, there is no us. Thank you.

ABOUT THE AUTHORS

Andy King is a bakery owner and former freelance food writer. He graduated with a degree in Music from Colby College (Waterville, Maine), shortly thereafter attending the New England Culinary Institute (Montpelier, Vermont) where he met his wife to-be and partner, Jackie. Andy spent a season at the James Beard Award-winning restaurant Arrows (Ogunquit, Maine) before moving to the baking world. After 3 ½ years training at Maine's premier artisan bakery, the Standard Baking Co. (Portland, Maine), he and Jackie opened A&J King Artisan Bakers (Salem, Massachusetts) in 2006. He lives in Topsfield, Massachusetts with Jackie, their two children and a rotating cast of animals.

Jackie King attended the New England Culinary Institute (Montpelier, Vermont) where she met her husband to-be, Andy. After working as chef for Nasturtium (Newburyport, Massachusetts), she trained for 3 ½ years at Maine's premier artisan bakery, the Standard Baking Co. (Portland, Maine). She and Andy opened A&J King Artisan Bakers (Salem, Massachusetts) in 2006. She lives in Topsfield, Massachusetts with Andy, their two children and a rotating cast of animals.

SOURCES

Many of the items used in this book can be purchased at your local hardware store or box homeware stores. Sticky bun tins, measuring spoons, digital scales and the like are fairly easily had. For those other things that might not be available locally, check these places out. They're the suppliers that we deal with, and should have everything you need.

www.bakedeco.com

Cake circles/circle cutters, tart rings, large rolling pins . . . This Brooklyn-based supplier will have just about everything you need for your pastry creations, and a few bread items as well. Their bakeware section is enormous and comprehensive.

www.tmbbaking.com

Bannetons, lames, razors, peels . . . TMB, located in San Francisco, is a wonderful supplier of artisan bread equipment. They'll even help you get started if you decide to open your own bakery!

www.bbga.org

The Bread Baker's Guild of America. For those of you serious about your bread, the Guild offers regional classes, informational workshops, a fantastic newsletter packed with recipes and advice and a community of like-minded bakers who have probably encountered any problem you could come up with.

INDEX